THE INTELLIGENT EYE

REALITY RE-SEEN

recent paintings by
WILLIAM BAGGETT

Published in conjunction with the travelling exhibition
The Intelligent Eye – Reality Re-Seen,
Recent Paintings by William Baggett

Foreword and essay by *Renata Karlin, Ph.D.*

Distributed by *University Press of Mississippi*

Museum Director, *Jan L. Siesling*
Museum of Art, SS Box 5033
The University of Southern Mississippi
Hattiesburg, MS 39406

Exhibition Coordinator, *Susan Fitzsimmons*
Graphic Design, *Lynne J. Baggett (Bzquare Editions)*

Printed and bound in China. First printing 2010

Front cover: *Menace*, oil on panel, 18" x 14", 2008

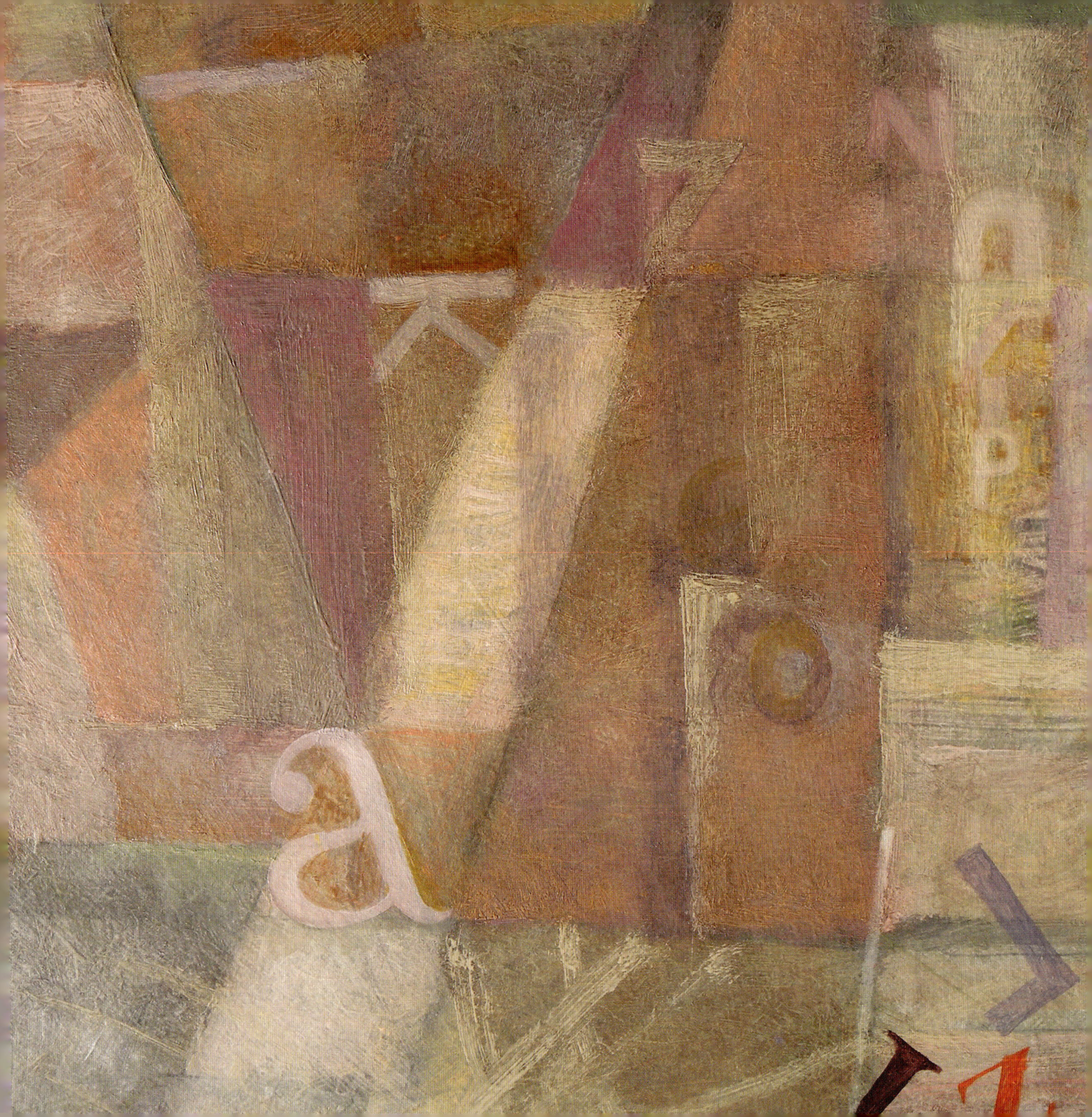

THE INTELLIGENT EYE

REALITY RE-SEEN

recent paintings by
WILLIAM BAGGETT

CONTENTS

Opposite: *Sleeping Quarry* (detail), oil on panel, 20" x 16", 2008

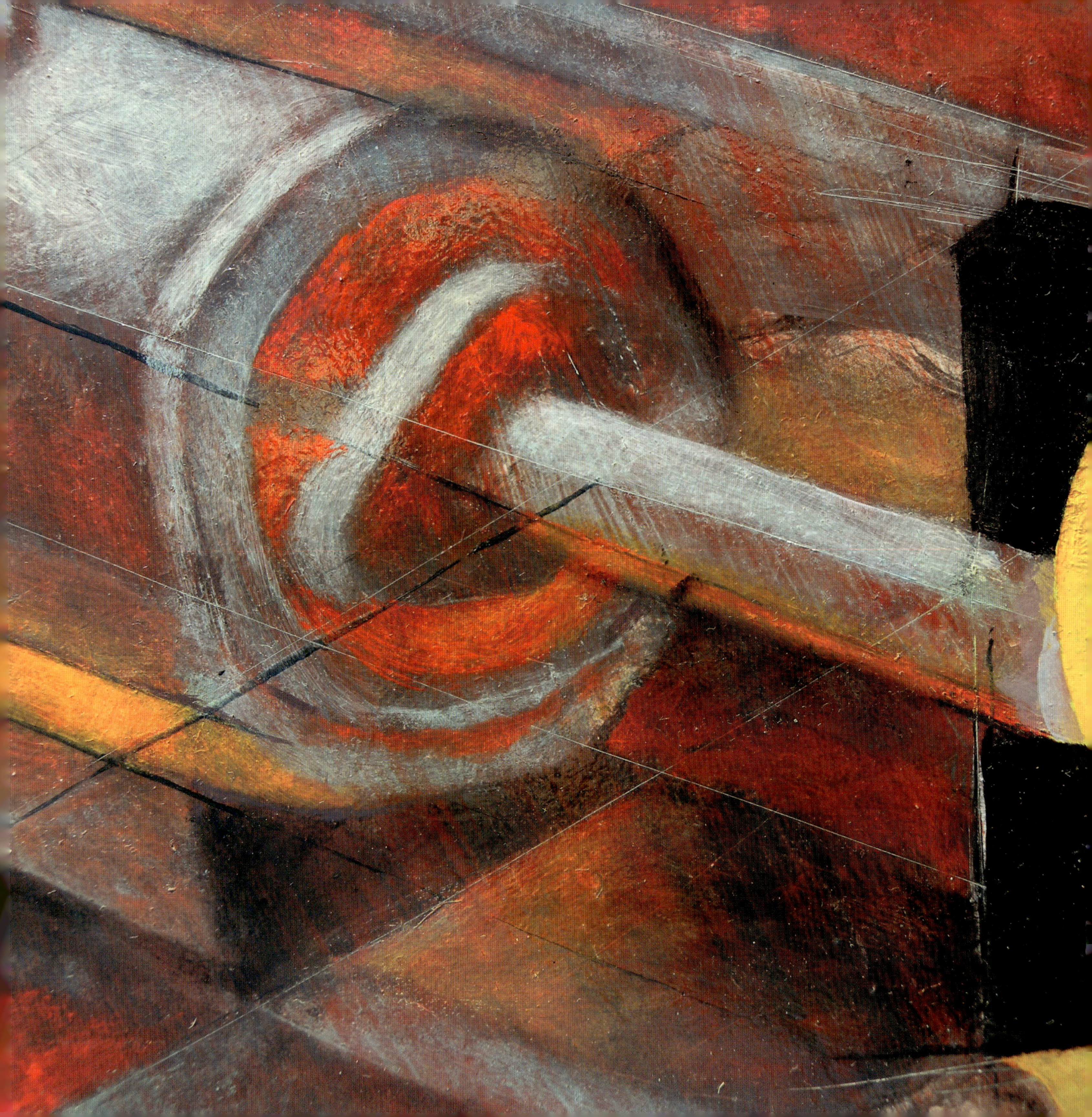

FOREWORD BY RENATA KARLIN

A GREAT DEAL OF ART CRITICISM

is written in terms of our expectations about what constitutes accepted sensibility and acceptable visual language at a given moment in time. We know that the visual language of art in the 20th century was dominated by varying degrees of independence from visual references to the world.

Until recently, the artistic assessment of a 20th century artist always depended upon the criteria to define modernism, seen primarily as a process of increasing reduction. Minimalism or Conceptual Art seemed to confirm reductionism as a historical necessity so that the abstract picture or sculpture disappeared in the name of dematerialization.

Preoccupation with pictorial conventions can easily blind one to the actual experience of seeing. Re-seeing, the simultaneity of vision and perception, allows our expectation and ideas of acceptability to regroup, revise and reorganize themselves and allows us to see again with new eyes.

One of the artists, whose legacy has undergone such re-evaluation, is Giorgio Morandi (1890-1964). Morandi, who painted mostly simple everyday objects—he arranged bottles, vases, vessels and jugs in ever-new compositions or painted the view out of his studio window from different angles— was admired by fellow artists, dismissed by some as an Italian regionalist and disparagingly called a "bottle painter" by his fiercest critics. He lived quietly earning his living mostly through teaching. The significance of the re-evaluation of Morandi's place in the history of art can be measured by the large number of one-person retrospectives in major international museums featuring his paintings, watercolors and etchings.

Baggett, like Morandi, paints everyday objects. He has been called "traditional" and "conservative", sometimes labeled a "Southern regionalist".

"HE MAKES US REASSESS OUR RELATIONSHIP TO REALITY, THE FABRIC OF THE WORLD AROUND US. "

Like Morandi, he makes us reassess our relationship to reality, the fabric of the world around us. Nature to Baggett is not bound to any fixed order and thus the Renaissance tradition of atmospheric perspective, organizing a painting into sequences of receding pictorial space, no longer applies. In its place is a thoroughly modernist vision of painterly space as an element that evolves during the process of creating. In all his work, the separation of the figure from the realm of objects allows the picture to be seen as a deliberate arrangement of forms in which plane and space interact and space becomes indistinguishable from the object.

Opposite: *Vapor (detail),* oil on panel, 21" x 19", 2007

As with Morandi, Baggett has been able to earn his living through teaching, which allowed him to pursue his art without heeding critics who might wish him to be either more abstract or more realistic. It also allowed him to build a reputation—primarily in the South—independent from the conventional art establishment. It would be a formidable task to identify all his works scattered throughout public and private collections.

A one-person show of Baggett's work is appropriate and timely in light of the general re-evaluation

FIG. 1. *Walking,* watercolor on paper, 26" x 20", 1973

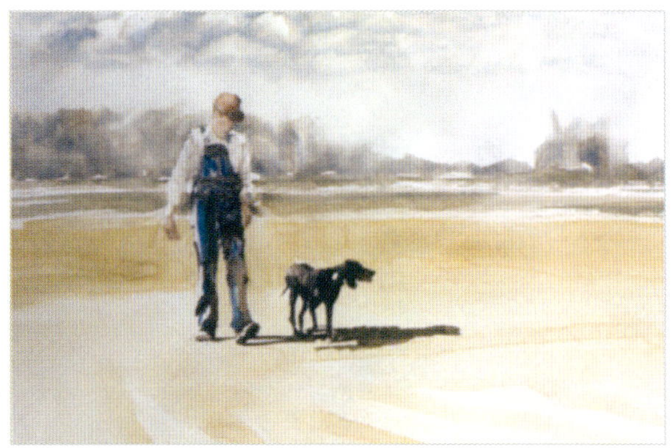

of the role and the relationship of realism and abstraction in contemporary art. On the surface, the large body of his output has been representational and figurative; a solitary figure frequently featured in his work. In this early watercolor, entitled *Walking* (FIG. 1) for instance, a solitary male figure is depicted walking with his dog on—what appears to be—a dirt road or a flat field. At first glance, both the figures and the landscape are deceptively realistic but there is a slight sense of inappropriateness. The figure, although clearly walking, is arrested as if trapped in thought and the perspective of the figure, accentuated by the shadow cast by man and dog, is not aligned with the landscape; not significantly enough to be immediately obvious but nevertheless disquietingly challenging. The figures are deliberately accentuated shapes set against a landscape depicted through seemingly spontaneous patches of color. The double nature of this watercolor—to consist of pictorial elements and to show forms through fluctuation between surface and depth—shows Baggett's indebtedness to Cezanne and puts him squarely in the company of almost every artist of the 20th century. Cezanne's process of "controlled seeing", i.e., seeing nature anew continuously as a manifestation of space, light, color and forms, allowed painting to become an operation of autonomous elements in which visible things are descriptively realized.

A watercolor, painted a few years later, entitled *Relic* (FIG. 2), makes Baggett's artistic vision more explicit. The title itself is—in his words—"a good lie". It induces the uninitiated viewer to look for a story, to believe that the painting depicts something recognizable or "real". The vertical cluster of men, articulated through the light-dark contrasting of their clothing, is placed almost precipitously in the upper right-hand corner on a field, whose upward curving plowed grooves create a perspective incongruous with the horizontality of the spontaneous patches of color with the trees on the horizon.

For Baggett "every conscious decision in painting is about form", where a particular shape or form is placed in the organization of the pictorial space. He employs the structural world of forms, landscapes, figures and buildings to seduce the viewer to enter the pictorial space. He evokes visually recognizable forms to create a sense of reality and thus familiarity, so that the viewer can begin to appreciate the artist's pictorial intent.

The sense of familiarity invoked by his paintings is one of the reasons why his work was shown for several years in conjunction with the annual William Faulkner symposium at the University of Mississippi. Many of his paintings from the 70's and 80's evoked images somewhat reminiscent of the traditional South, as for instance, a watercolor, entitled *Oyster Fantasy* (FIG. 3). The figure in the doorway, positioned slightly off-center, is the only organic shape in the unrelenting alignment of

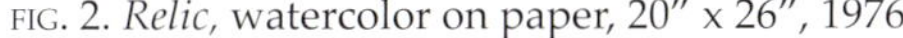

FIG. 2. *Relic,* watercolor on paper, 20" x 26", 1976

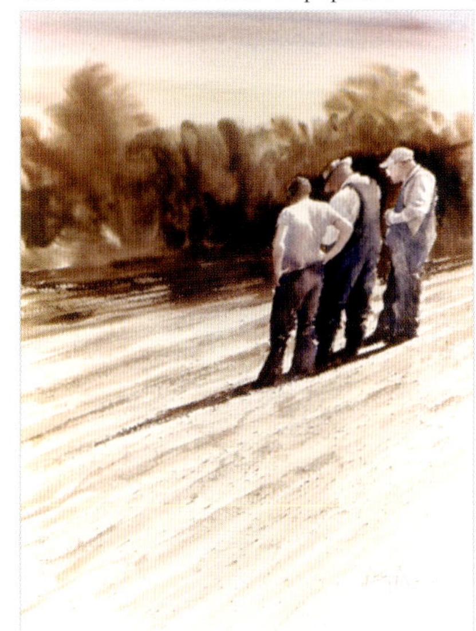

rectangular, architectural shapes and lines both vertically and horizontally. The shadowy figure would easily be overlooked were it not for a shaft of light, which arrow-like points down from the roof to the feet of the figure.

"THE SHADOWY FIGURE WOULD EASILY BE OVERLOOKED WERE IT NOT FOR A SHAFT OF LIGHT"

As Baggett's utilization of pictorial space matured, the undulation between surface and depth became more deliberate and more pronounced. It is not surprising therefore that for several years he immersed himself in the medium of egg tempera painting, a technique which forced a "kind of pre-

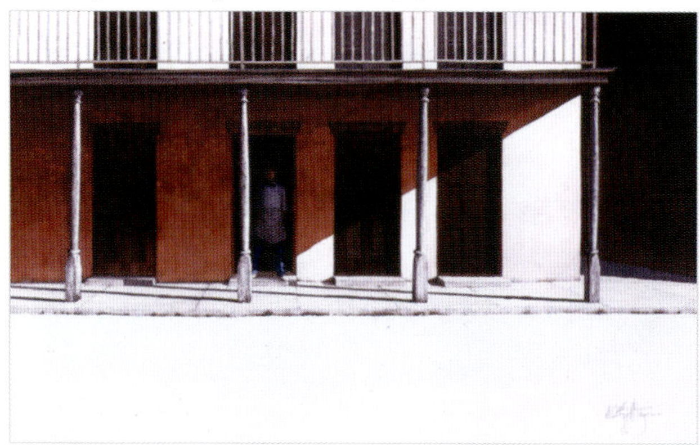

FIG. 3. *Oyster Fantasy,* watercolor on paper, 24" x 18", 1978

engineering". In the painting, entitled **Tempest** (FIG. 4), Baggett achieves physical depth by the build-up of many layers of crosshatched brush strokes applied in alternatively warm and cool colors. The result is a build-up of color, which the eye blends optically as a softened chromatic effect on a luminous and opalescent surface.

In a catalog introduction to a 1991 exhibition of his egg tempera paintings, Baggett spoke about wishing "to create illogical juxtapositions of the figure with various objects in the painting and with the boundaries of the composition." The two-fold reading of the picture, has led critics to connect his work with "magic realism" and the Southern tradition of "storytelling". However, Baggett's work is neither about telling a story or magic, or reality. The female figure in this egg tempera series is not a portrait. She is a prop for Baggett to manipulate the painterly space, as are the objects that define the interior against which she is posed.

Painting to Baggett is about a way of seeing and about the role of pictorial elements with the intent of—in his words—"creating a situation where everything is posed and becomes significant." The separation of the figure from the anticipated realm of the objects allows the picture to be seen as a deliberate arrangement of forms in which plane and space interact and space become indistinguishable from the object.

The discipline of egg tempera painting, the deliberate building up and blending of shapes and colors provided a challenge and an opportunity for Baggett to see whether he could achieve what he had intended—"boxing myself 'in' so that I could test my ability to escape successfully".

Boxing himself "in" was probably a significant motivation for Baggett in challenging himself to create four mural oil paintings between 1993 and 2004, the largest of which, a panoramic painting 10 by 167 feet in circumference (imagine the inside of a truncated cone), can be viewed some 30 feet above the main circulation desk of The Library of Hattiesburg, Petal and Forrest County.

The mural, entitled, *The Spirit that Builds* (FIG. 5), is Baggett's depiction of the social history of Hattiesburg and its environment. Painted on a sand-blasted stainless steel surface with artist-grade alkyd, fast-drying oil paint, the execution of the mural, occupied Baggett for almost three years. (The first year was devoted to historical research. During the second year the concepts were drawn full size on preliminary 12-feet square paper panels experimenting with the flow of historical sequences).

The mural created both challenges and opportunities for the artist. Principal among the challenges was the monumentality of the "canvas" and the resultant duration of the project; which included ongoing collaboration with many individuals to permit the artist to maintain his schedule.

The artistic opportunities offered in this project were manifold and varied. The panoramic, circular structure of the mural calls for a chronologically sequential narrative. One challenge was to keep the illusion of chronology while allowing the visual elements to be both aspects of the visual world as

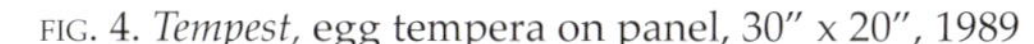

"*CREATING A SITUATION WHERE EVERYTHING IS POSED AND BECOMES SIGNIFICANT*"

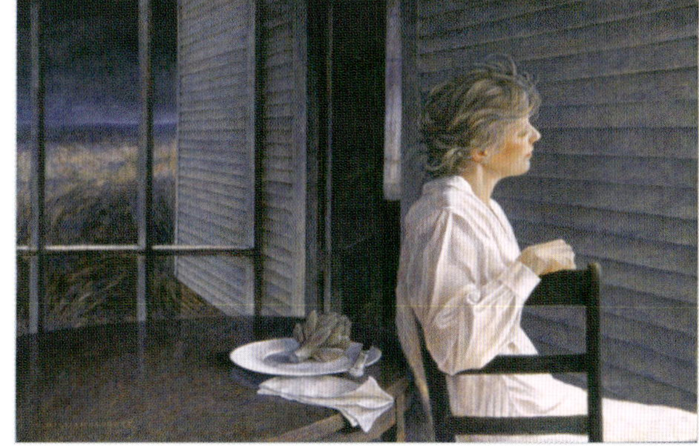

FIG. 4. *Tempest,* egg tempera on panel, 30" x 20", 1989

"SKILLED OSCILLATION BETWEEN SURFACE AND DEPTH"

well as creative devices. Baggett jams the scenes together in such a way that natural subjects could in reality not exist in such proximity, yet he forces them into a "sufficiently convincing order so that the viewer wants to believe it." He achieves this by his skilled oscillation between surface and depth, keeping the eye moving from left to right, front to back from one visual prop to the next, as if the whole panorama revolves and undulates like a chronological carousel of color and form.

Typically, monumental works call for a kind of freezing of images, which accounts for their tendency toward stiffness. Instead of stiffness however, we experience an arrested calmness in **The Spirit that Builds**. The human figures, trees,

FIG. 5. *The Spirit That Builds,* alkyd oil on stainless steel, 10' x 167', 1995

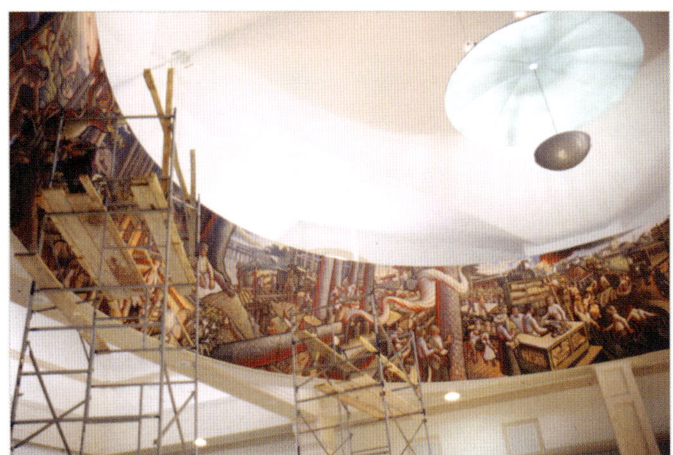

agricultural and industrial operations, machines and buildings, are all allotted the same pictorial significance, ignoring physical properties such as the hardness of a physical material, the texture of a surface, etc. They share equally in the allotment of space, light, color and form. By giving landscape, human figures, buildings and machines the same visual value, Baggett has successfully avoided making this mural either a historical, sociological account or an idealized mythological presentation. It is simply his view of reality shaped into an integrated whole.

Calm deliberateness has always been a notable feature of Baggett's work. It allowed him to depict "reality" in which the presence of objects and figures and the steadfastness of the world is questioned so that the viewer can appreciate his true pictorial intent in organizing pictorial space, where every decision is about the deliberate arrangement of forms in which plane and space interact and space becomes indistinguishable from the forms.

Bolstered by the security of various academic appointments, Baggett has been able to pursue his artistic vision in relative obscurity, choosing the way of "quietism, of willed obscurity, of inner immigration" [1]

1. J.M. COETZEE, *Diary of a Bad Year,* Penguin Books 2008, ISBN 978-0-14-311448-2, p.12

AFTER SUCCESSFULLY IMPRINTING his pictorial concepts on the panoramic mural at the Hattiesburg Public Library, as well as three additional figurative murals (a mural, commissioned by The University of Southern Mississippi, another by the Jule Collins Smith Museum of Fine Art at Auburn University, Alabama, and one in Jackson, Mississippi, commissioned by the University of Mississippi Medical Center), Baggett did not pursue the mural genre any further. However, the twelve-year intense immersion with artist-grade alkyd oil paint (an oil color made from pigment and oil modified alkyd resin as opposed to traditional linseed-based oil paint), left a profound visceral imprint his palette. He became enamored with the alkyd oil's luminosity and translucency and its more predictable drying time, which maximized the opportunity for multiple layers of color glazing.

When Baggett was ready to return to the smaller, rectangular pictorial space he had worked with for most of his life, it was only logical that he would extend his exploration with alkyd oil pigments. And a life-long familiarity with manipulating color and shapes on a flat rectangle provided the opportunity to develop a more intimate and personal iconography. The oil paintings shown in this exhibit are the work of a master who has matured and has come home to himself, like a dancer who has mastered his technique to the point where the piece performs itself.

Let us look at one of the earliest works in this series, entitled *Avocado Economy* (PLATE 1). The carefully calibrated relationship between lines, spaces and objects are employed to pull things apart as well as bring them together. The painting does not direct but disperses our attention and invites us to investigate and navigate through its spatial construction. Dense layering of warm and cool colors create a flowing transition between pictorial planes. For Baggett, form and space become something to be apportioned during the execution of a painting.

Baggett refers to these painting as "just my personal musings" and lightheartedly describes them as "really selfish work." Frequently, as in **Avocado Economy,** he starts with a dark background color onto which he delineates an informal grid, which he further breaks up and develops into unspecified shapes. Baggett reaches deep into his subconscious visual memory to develop these shapes. He likens the process to looking at clouds, "you pull a little here, a bit there, push here; it evolves." Eventually, the shapes begin to suggest specific objects: the greenish ovals along the left corner frame reveal themselves as avocados and the interlocking triangles and rectangles in the middle are shaped into an accordion-folded piece of paper; with the number "1" added at the edges suggesting a folded one dollar bill—hence the ironic title. The repeated and inverted numbers "2" and the letter "z" clearly silhouetted against a dark background, together with the wave patterns, evoke a fluttering motion as if they produce a current that makes the dollar bill flutter and almost fly out of the picture. This adds to the vacillation between surface and depth and the flowing transition between pictorial planes. The reader is caught in the two-fold reading of the picture: reading the arrangements of the forms, we also read their convertibility and vice versa.

Because the painting depicts recognizable shapes incongruously placed on other shapes on the picture plane, one might be tempted to read these oil paintings as a variant of surrealism. Nothing could be further from the truth. As mentioned earlier, for Baggett "every conscious decision in painting is about form"; how and where a particular shape or form is placed in the organization of the pictorial space. These shapes, as were the figures in his earlier work, are devices to induce the viewer to enter the pictorial space and navigate through his pictorial arrangement of shapes, forms and colors.

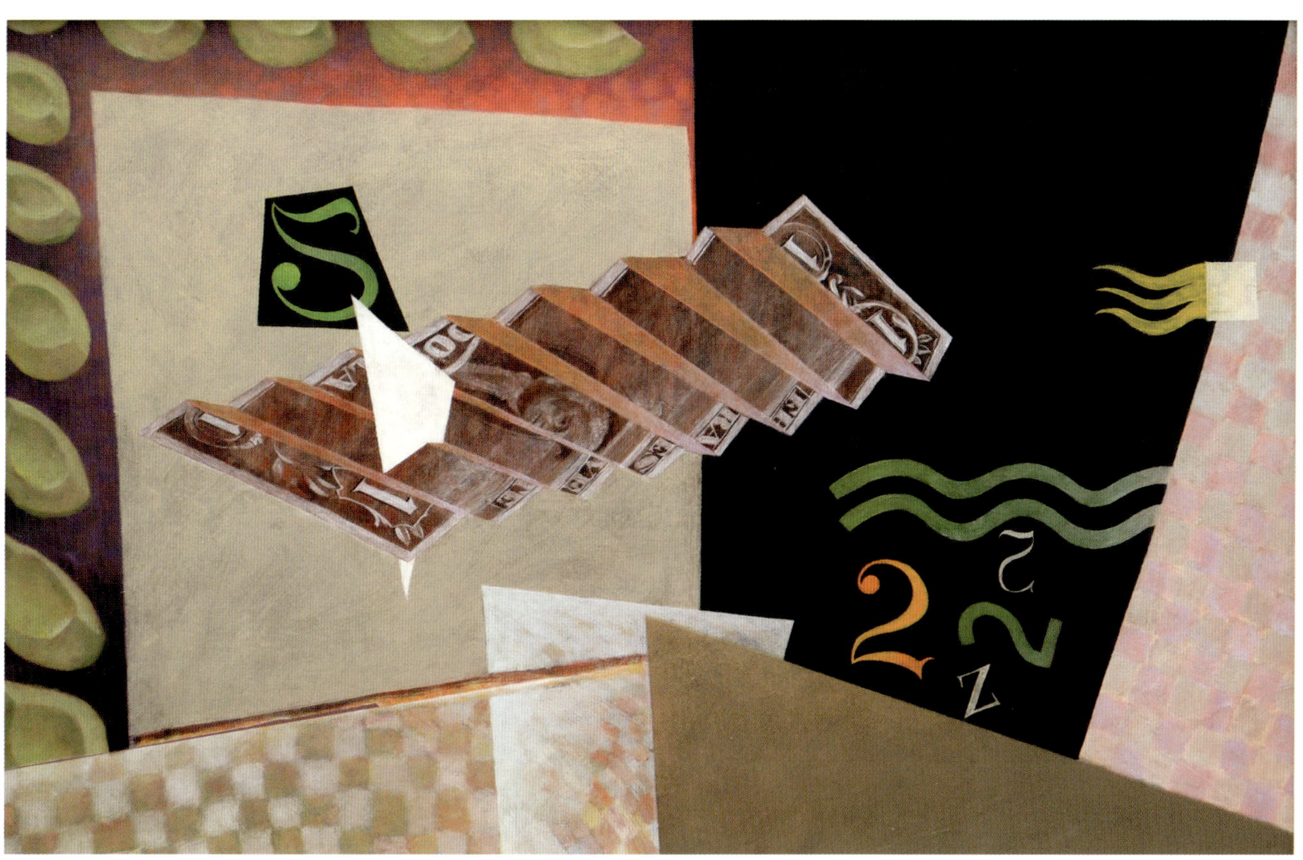

PLATE I. *Avocado Economy*, 36″ x 24″

The use of color also adds to the fluctuation between surface and depth. The shapes of the "dollar bill" overlap the dark flat shape on the right as well as a translucent salmon-colored rectangle on the left, so that the dollar bills floats like a magic carpet through and over the picture. Baggett achieves the softened chromatic effect of the surfaces by building up layers through crosshatched brush strokes reminiscent of the technique he used in his egg tempera paintings. Careful reading reveals the same chromatic effect throughout the pictorial space. The result is a luminescent and opalescent surface, particularly evident in the lighter and warmer colors, such as in the triangular, checkered shape on the right and on the slightly darker colored rectangle intersecting the lower left corner. The fluttering motion of the numbers and waves is accentuated through the same warm/cool layering of colors.

Chromatic layering, translucency and opalescence are very much evident in a painting from the same period, entitled **Menace** (PLATE II). The pictorial space is occupied by clearly defined, geometric and organic shapes: orange globes at the right that could also be seen as a small grove of trees; the large rounded melon shape in the middle that could be a hill, and the pointed grayish shapes on the left evoke a veritable forest of asparagus tips. Whatever their original intent, they are essentially organic as opposed to the rigid geometry of the triangular and rectangular shapes. The organic shapes are isolated, liberated from their natural existence, enlarged or otherwise altered lending them a different intensity and presence (hence the title). The "asparagus tips" are highlighted in red as if bursting into flames, which—in the upper left corner—they seem to be in the process of doing. The yellow triangles overlapping the black triangle on the right evoke a folded cloth over a flat surface on which the "orange" forms are resting. The melon shape in the center of the pictorial space emerges as if surfacing from below and is highlighted by a luminescent spotlight-like triangle emerging from the upper right corner and its shape is silhouetted sharply in a violet circle, which is distorted, changes color and curved as it touches the blue spotlight.

Baggett uses space, light, and color to transform what he has stored in his visual memory into what he paints. Space, light, color, and form are aspect of the world around us, as well as creative means.

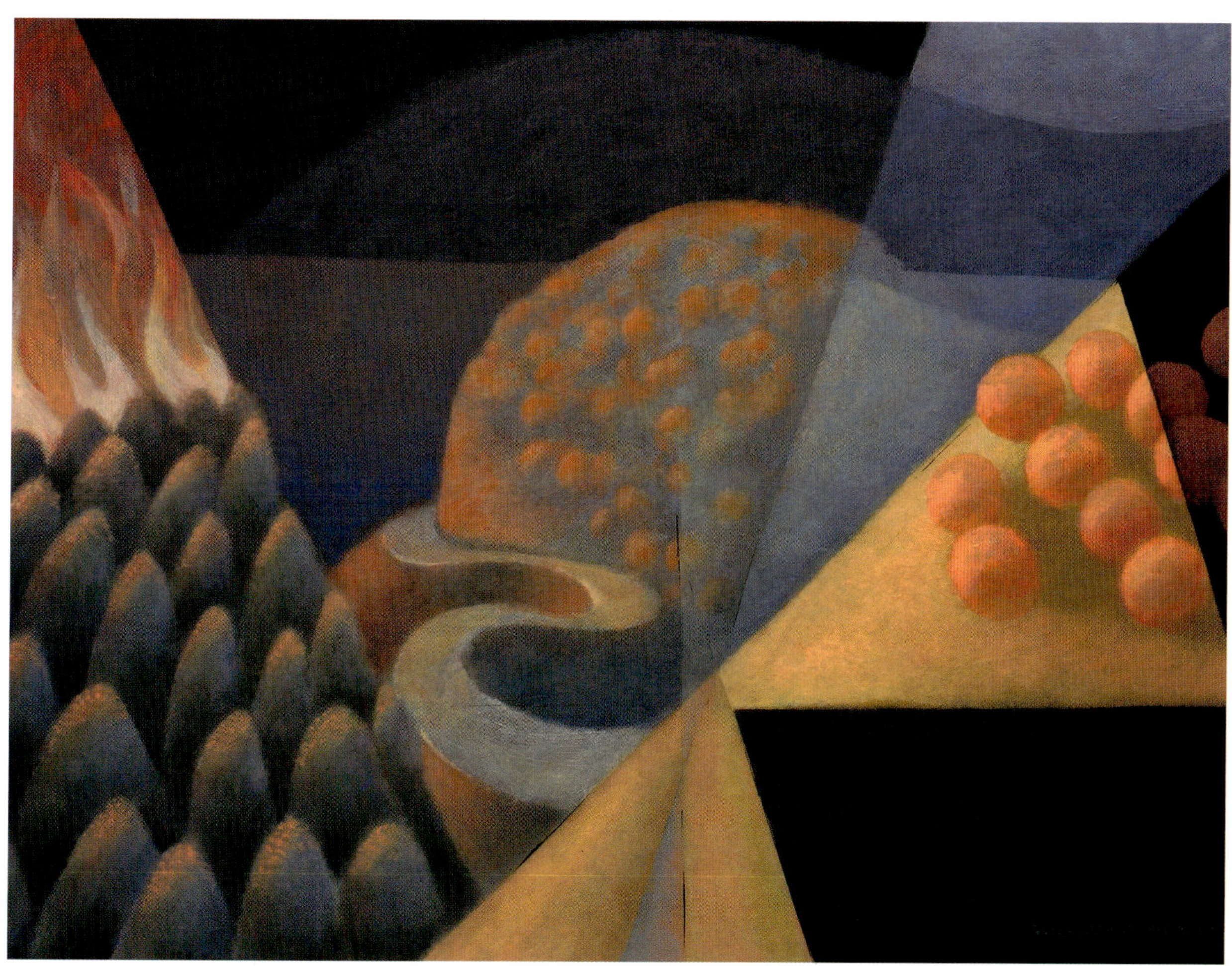

PLATE II. *Menace*, 18″ x 14″

Clearly defined shapes and a similar chromatic intensity is evident in *Passage* (PLATE III), part of a suite of paintings he began while summering in Maine. The apportioning of shapes and colors assigns clear allocations to foreground, background and in between. The color graduation and the fluidity of the blue shape in the center surrounded by more defined, darker and relatively hard-edged triangular and rectangular shapes, evokes a passage of water between rock formations, out to sea, and into a salmon-colored evening sky. The effect of the sky is evoked through positioning with the rusty shadowing of the light green rock-like shapes.

The colors have a brilliant luminescence as if they were lit from behind, something not evident in Baggett's earlier work. It is as if the wide-open sea and sky of Maine freed him from his Southern palette. The light in most of his previous work is filtered, dispersed, a warm light tending towards yellow, very much the light of the American South and Southwest. The layered build-up of colors of (what might be seen as) water and rocks and the added leaf-like shapes, creates a shimmering quality evoking more a feeling than an actual representation of a seascape.

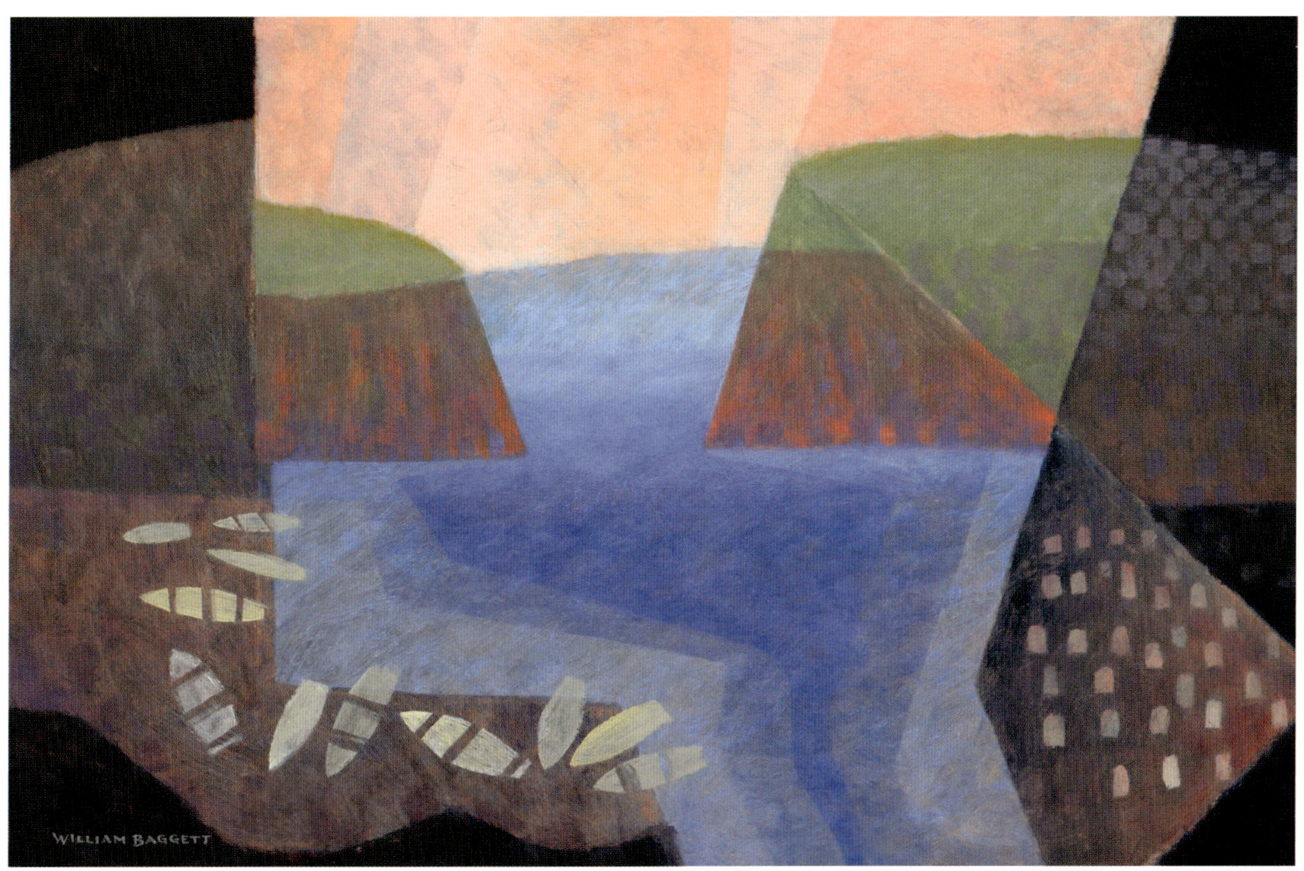

PLATE III. *Passage*, 24″ x 16″

Even without the title, the allocation of shapes in *Spotlighted Buoys* (PLATE IV), clearly assigns foreground, background and middle ground, evoking the feeling of a seascape. The same intense 'Northern light' luminescence prevails as in *Passage*. A brilliantly lighted red buoy shape, precariously tilted (to suggest heaving waves?), emerges from the center of the lower frame, its size and placement straining the verisimilitude of the seascape. A much smaller, grey-green silhouetted buoy is placed so close to the red one that it strains the verisimilitude of the spatial apportioning as does the vividly red quadrilateral shape behind it (to suggest another red buoy far away?).

There is a contagious sense of joy and fun in this painting. Baggett manipulates shapes and colors to make the viewer see something that is then denied as true, like the floating red number "2" on the red buoy, which is to some extent 'verified' as correct as it corresponds to the white number "1" on the smaller buoy, only to be put in question by the white inverted number "5" behind the "2". The scalloped patterns in the blue foreground morph into checkered patterns often used by Baggett, just so the viewer does not equate these patterns with waves.

It seems that the leisure of summer months to explore the use of the alkyd oils away from teaching responsibilities amid the sultry dampness of Mississippi; his immersion in the Northern landscape with its cool climate, bracing wind and brilliantly white light, allowed him to start fresh, create a new vision, a different iconography and freer pictorial language while—at the same time—fully harnessing his 40-plus years of artistic experience.

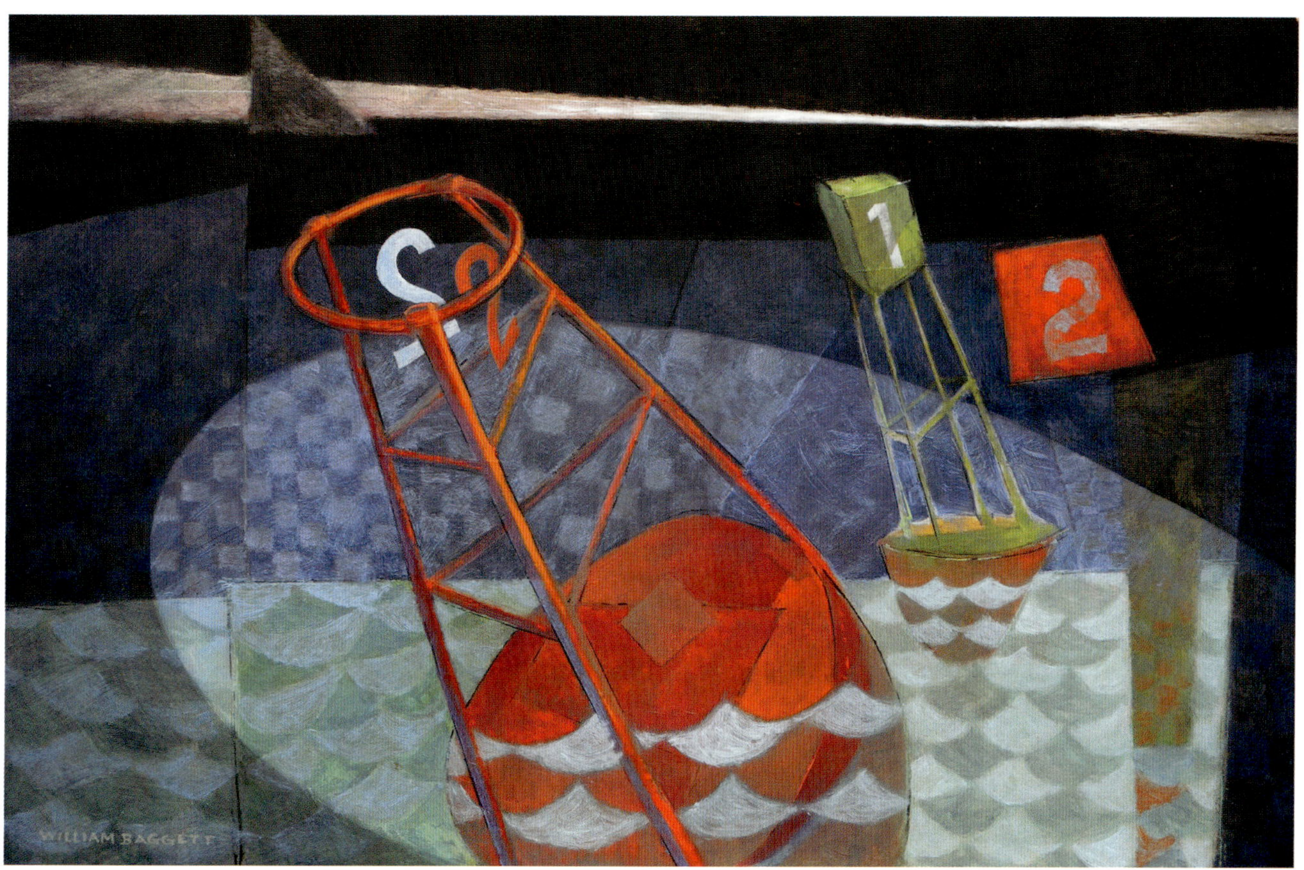

PLATE IV. *Spotlighted Buoys*, 24″ x 16″

A painting from the same period entitled *Crucible* (PLATE V) is a good example of Baggett's new pictorial vision and its title suggests that he was supremely conscious of the new direction in his work. One definition (according to Webster) of crucible is "a set of circumstances where people or things are subjected to forces that test them and often make them change." *Crucible* appears to have a similar seascape structure as **Passage**. Intersecting rectangular shapes, incongruously covered with different wave patterns pointing upwards, suggest water flowing toward the open sea. The juxtaposition of shapes and patterns creates a flowing transition between pictorial plane, eliminating the possibility of reading this painting as anything else but his deliberate apportioning of color, light, patterns and lines on the two-dimensional plane to suit his vision.

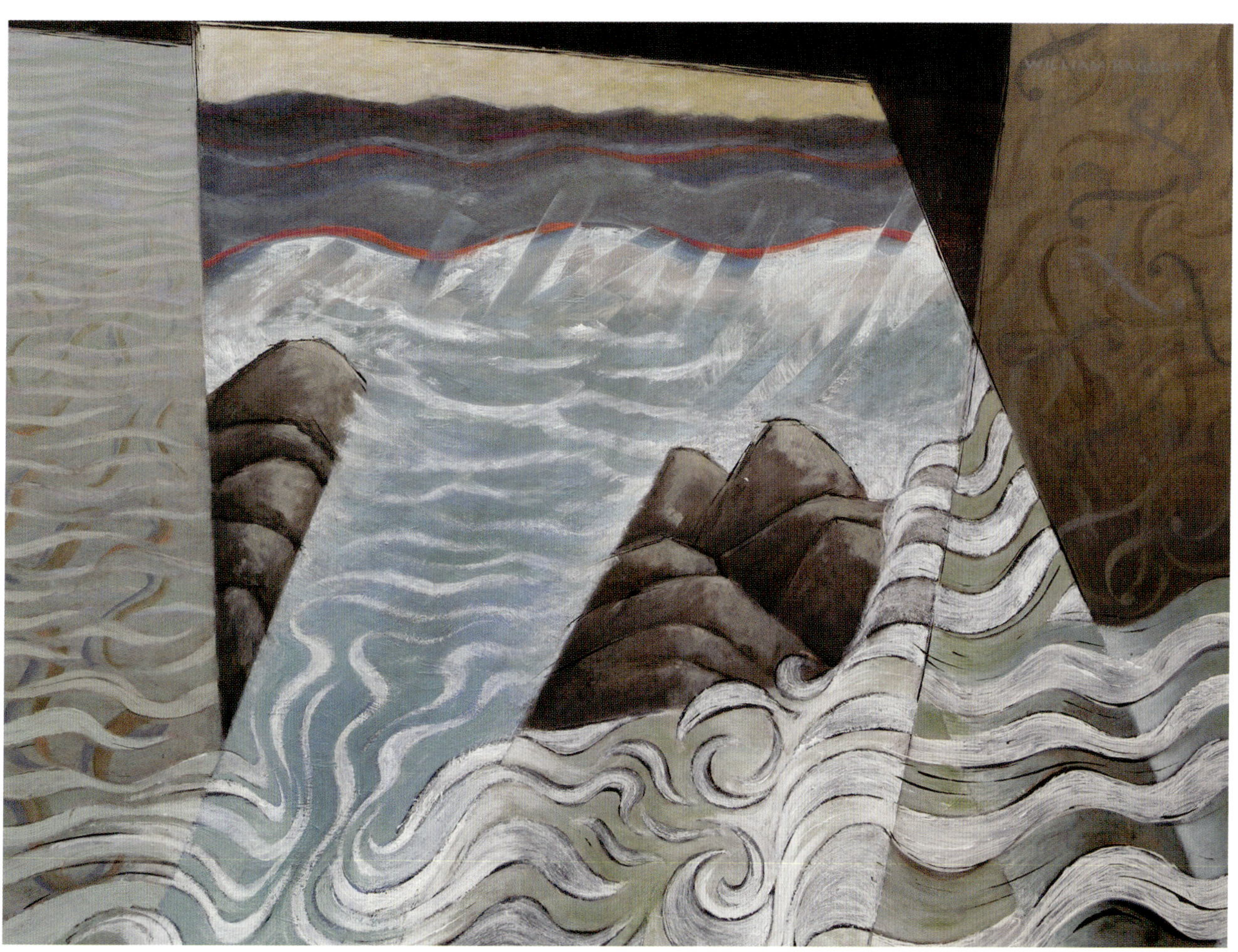

PLATE V. *Crucible*, 24″ x 18″

To summarize the visual intent underlying this series of paintings, a closer look at **Trolling for Bodoni** (PLATE VI) is in order. Completed at the end of a summer in Maine in 2008, the title, is a deceit, a "good lie". As such, the title encourages the viewer to look into the tackle box searching for something evoking "Bodoni". The viewer has been induced to accept the painting a representation of reality and yet, like Alice falling through the rabbit hole, the viewer realizes that this reality is not what it seems at first.

The overall translucent layering makes object appear as if seen through a slightly opaque layer of glass accentuating the oscillation between surface and depth. This forces the viewer to look more critically for "proof" that the tackle box exists, finding purchase perhaps in the rigorous alignment of colorful, rectangular shapes defining the box, only to discover that, despite alignment, nothing is aligned.

The box is precariously balanced on a platform that appears to be floating as are the lovingly rendered tackle and hooks positioned on the foreground. Their position suggests that the relevant story in the painting is happening beyond the picture frame and this is reinforced by the fact that the painting appears to be lit from three sources: from behind and two sides.

By this time the viewer may be assured that the letters floating above the tackle box like all the other lines and shapes and richly colored planes, are clues to simultaneously mislead and inform. The contradictions to linear perspective slow down our process of seeing and keep us off-balance by delineating objects and simultaneously keeping them at bay. The recognizable forms create a sense of reality, which lay bare Baggett's pictorial intent allowing the painting to be seen as a deliberate arrangement of forms, lines and color, imaginary constructions, rather than transcriptions of the world.

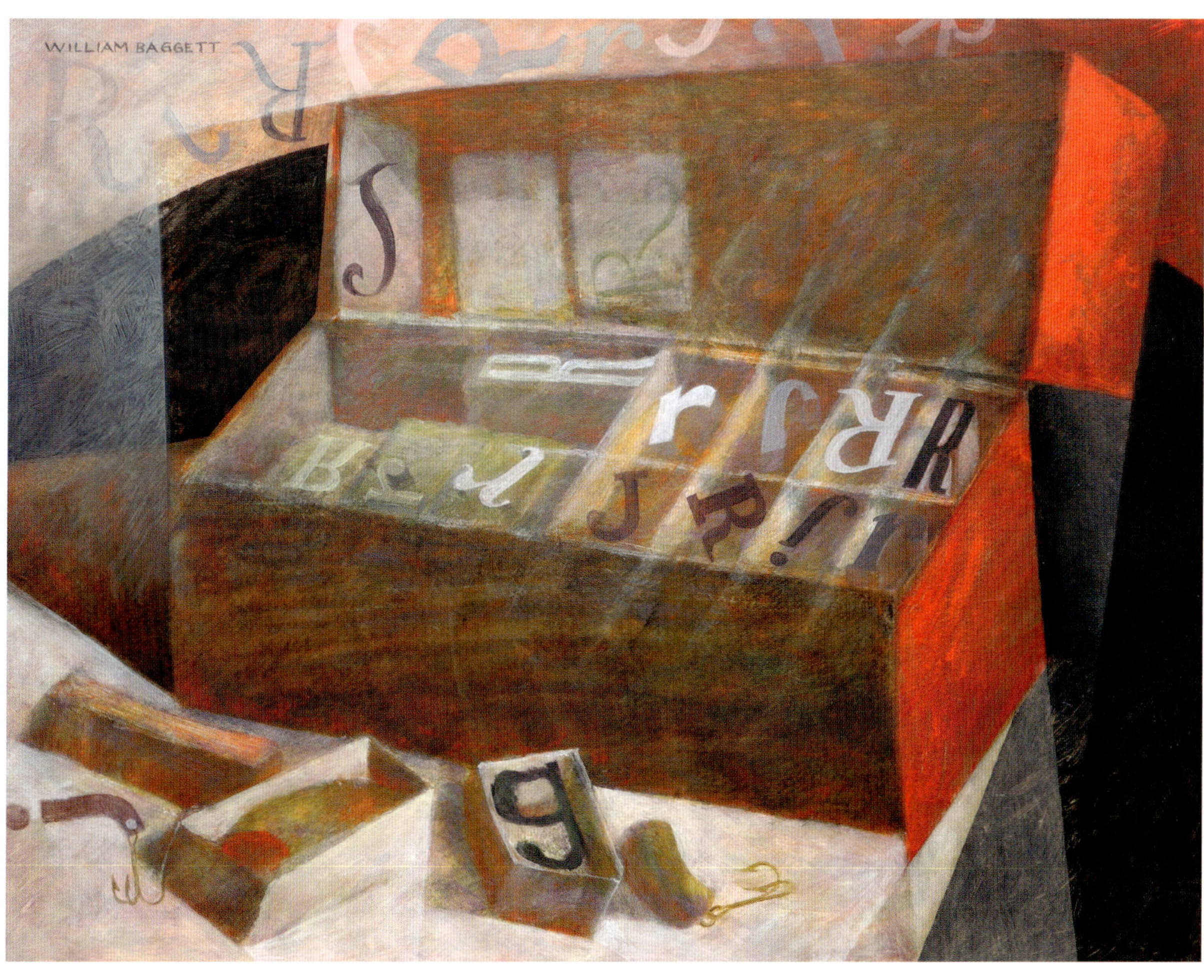

PLATE VI. *Trolling for Bodoni*, 20″ x 16″

In ***Overbearing Odds*** (PLATE VII), the temptation to see the work in the context of surrealism is more difficult to avoid. The clarity and almost monumental depiction of the forms evokes Matisse's search for the timeless absolute. However, the forms contain an emotional value absent in Matisse. The left side of the painting is dominated by an ominous dark object, almost hurling itself into the painting. The sense of calamity is reinforced by the raggedly folded object—perhaps evoking sea cliffs or a truncated set of stairs—projecting from the upper right down into the painting.

To anyone living on the Mississippi Gulf Coast in 2005 (as Baggett did), this shape immediately projects images from the aftermath of hurricane Katrina and the concomitant emotions related to total destruction and helplessness when faced with an overwhelming natural catastrophe. The title, reinforced by the depiction of seemingly random numbers on the dark object, suggests a speculation of the odds comparing a celestial object destroying earth to a hurricane destroying the Gulf Coast. The timeless absoluteness of the depiction is reinforced by the nearly square format of the painting.

The simplicity of the forms and spatial construction as well as the almost monumental clarity of the colors, only slightly moderated by the transparent rose color on the "cliffs" which is echoed in the sky above the celestial object, in no way diminishes the emotional impact experienced by both the viewer and the artist.

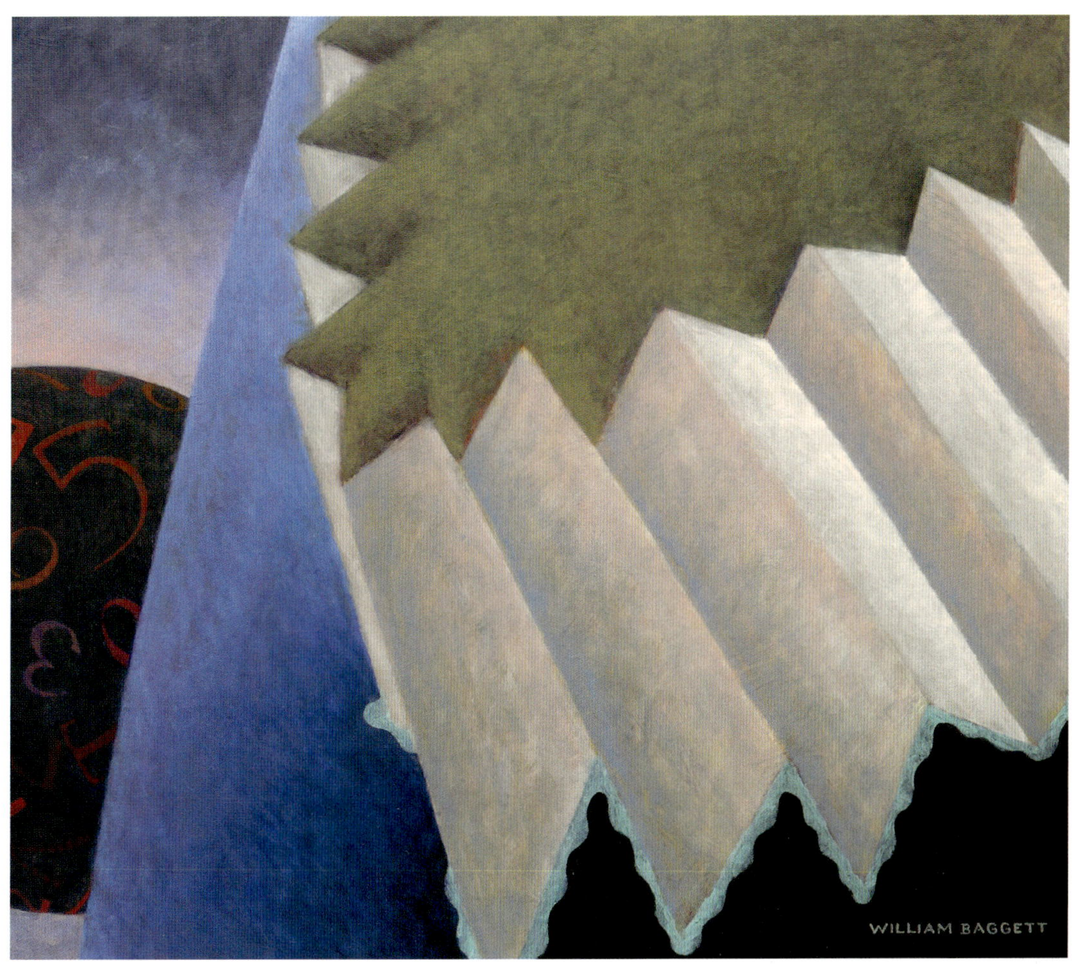

PLATE VII. *Overbearing Odds*, 22″ x 20″

Baggett's sense of calm deliberateness dominates *Narrows* (PLATE VIII). As the title suggests, the painting presents the illusion of a landscape and, as with most of the landscapes in this series, the rocky landscape of coastal Maine. The right side of this painting is not dissimilar to *Passage*, the apportioning of shapes and colors assigning clear allocations to foreground, background and in between, allowing the eye to believe that the narrowly curved strip of blue is a depiction of a narrow passage of water. The left side flatly contradicts this illusion. The round, many-layered red shape almost dominates the left side of the painting, particularly since it seems to rise ominously from below, evoking the melon-shaped form in *Menace*. The sharply triangular outcroppings on the upper left as well as the primarily black, totem-like shape adjoining the red and disappearing into the left side of the painting, undo any illusion that this is a landscape and force the viewer to acknowledge that this is an intricate spatial construction of shapes and forms, which through juxtaposition and dense layering of sometimes opaque, sometimes translucent colors achieves volume and depth.

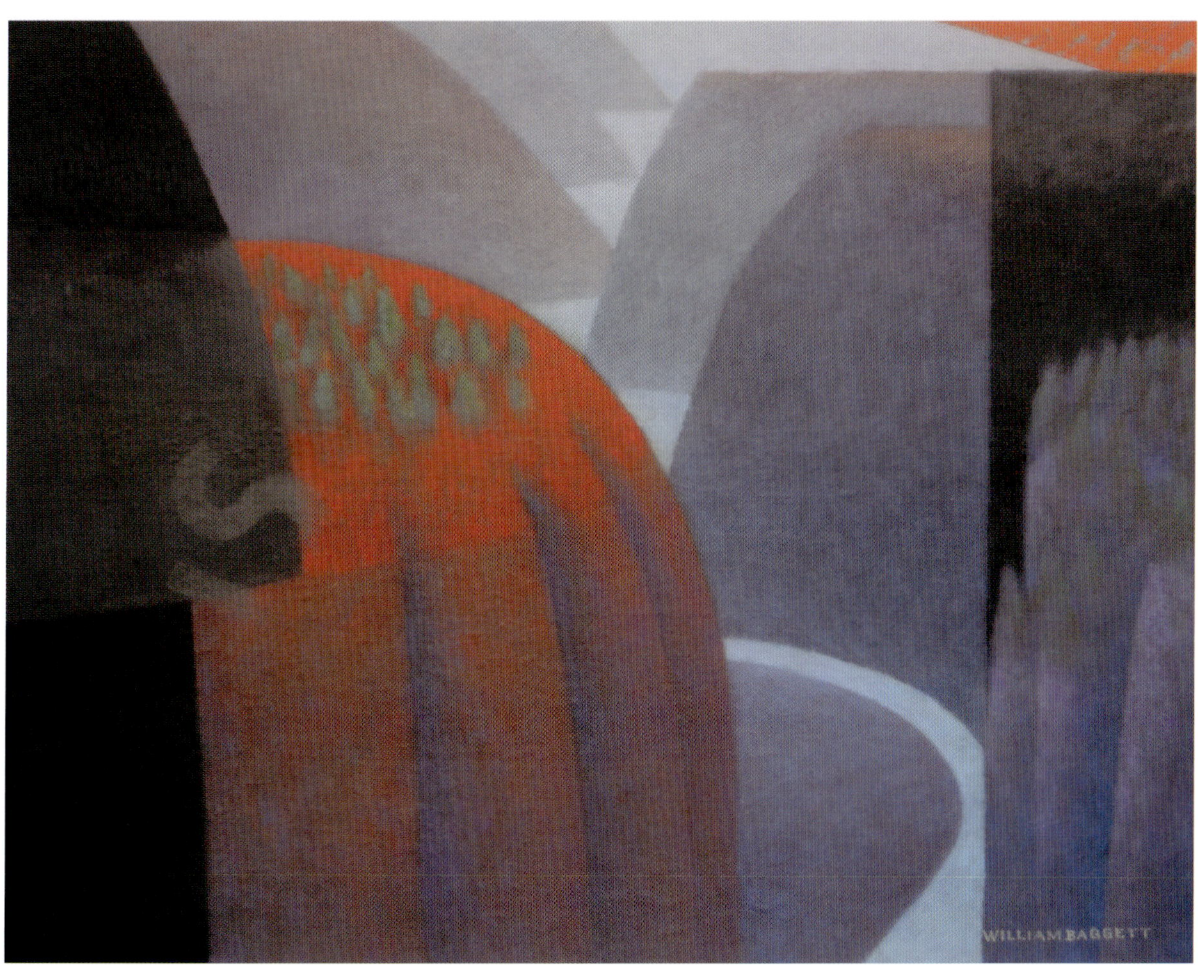

PLATE VIII. *Narrows*, 20″ x 16″

Like Minded (PLATE IX), one of four figurative paintings in the series, could be seen as an iconic portrait of two Maine lobstermen rising starkly against a background of unrelenting horizontality.

What makes this painting unique is that, unlike the other paintings in this series, which evolve in the process of painting, this painting appears to be "pre-engineered" (different from, but with similar intent as in his earlier egg tempera paintings). The use of geometric shapes (cone, globe and column) to depict the figures, is almost cubist. The use of the number "5" to depict facial anatomy as well as the division of the painting into horizontal bands evokes a much earlier "cubist": Piero della Francesca, one of the earliest and most original artists of the Renaissance. Piero had two passions: art and mathematics. He explored both at the same time and, as a teacher and practitioner, sought to establish the link between the organic and the geometric basis of beauty (Kenneth Clark called it "the Philosophers stone of aesthetics").

Seen through this aesthetic lens, *Like Minded*, rather than an idealized portrait of a pair of fisher-men, can be seen as a meticulously executed, personalized exercise in the simplification of human anatomy into the same elemental geometric forms used to depict the surrounding space. The juxtaposition of organic and geometric shapes prevalent in all of Baggett's work can now be more easily seen as his unique aesthetic stance that reflects a specific personal preoccupation, not unlike that of Piero.

Baggett describes his personal sensibilities toward geometry and linear perspective as "…essential conventions that must be thoroughly understood in order to be twisted to suit one's own needs."

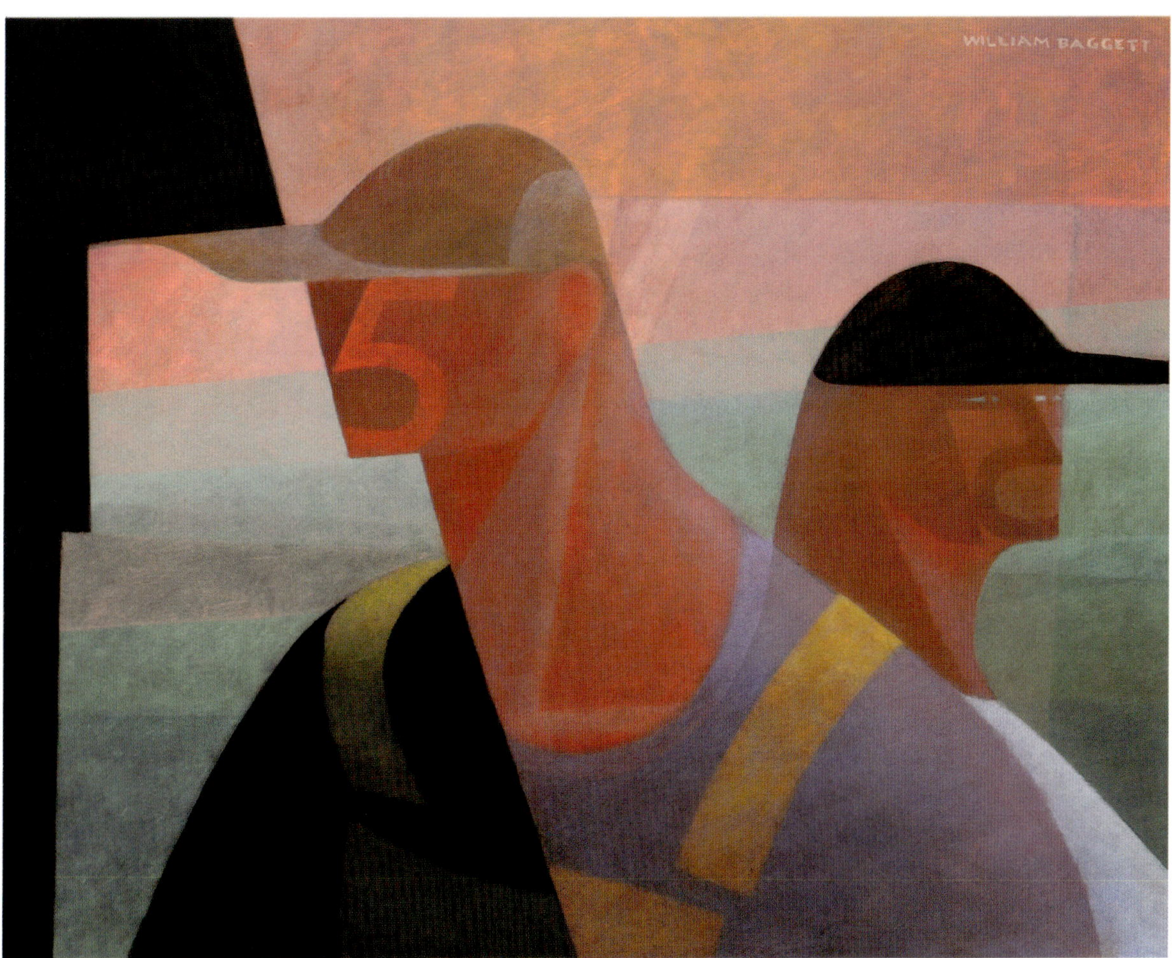

PLATE IX. *Like Minded*, 22″ x 18″

In ***Mammatus Birth*** (PLATE X), organic and geometric shapes are not linked but juxtaposed and sectioned off between the upper and lower and part of the painting. The vertically rectangular composition is unusual for Baggett, who favors to paint on a square or nearly square, often horizontal canvas. Pouch-like mammary clouds (also referred to as breast clouds) are relatively rare phenomena and, for this reason, as well as for their at times ominous appearance, are seen as predictors of severe weather conditions.

By contrast, these bulbous forms, beautifully lit from below, have the airiness and exuberance seen in Mannerist or Baroque paintings. Even without the title, the V-shaped opening from which the clouds emerge suggests an inverted female torso. The pink-dappled ribbon, seemingly holding the "torso" together as well as the opaque and translucent layering of the blue triangles and rectangles defining the "torso", softens and transmutes the seemingly rigid geometric shapes linking them to the richly organic appearance of the mammatus clouds.

The casual viewer might not fully appreciate the art-historical "lessons" imbedded in this painting, but surely will intuit the "lesson" in perspective and appreciate the degree of meticulous care with which Baggett sets up his constructs. Perhaps it is Baggett's experience of teaching art in an academic setting or perhaps it is simply an unconscious expression of what he has learned.

Whatever the impetus, one aspect of this particular series of oil paintings is that they feel like a tutorial about what it means to put oil on canvas in the post-modern world. Ever since the high Renaissance, an important aspect of painting was about creating the illusion of a three-dimensional world, the illusion of "reality" by making the viewer see depth and volume on a flat surface. By the late 19th century the classical perspectival practice was codified in the salon painters and ripe for challenge by the Impressionists.

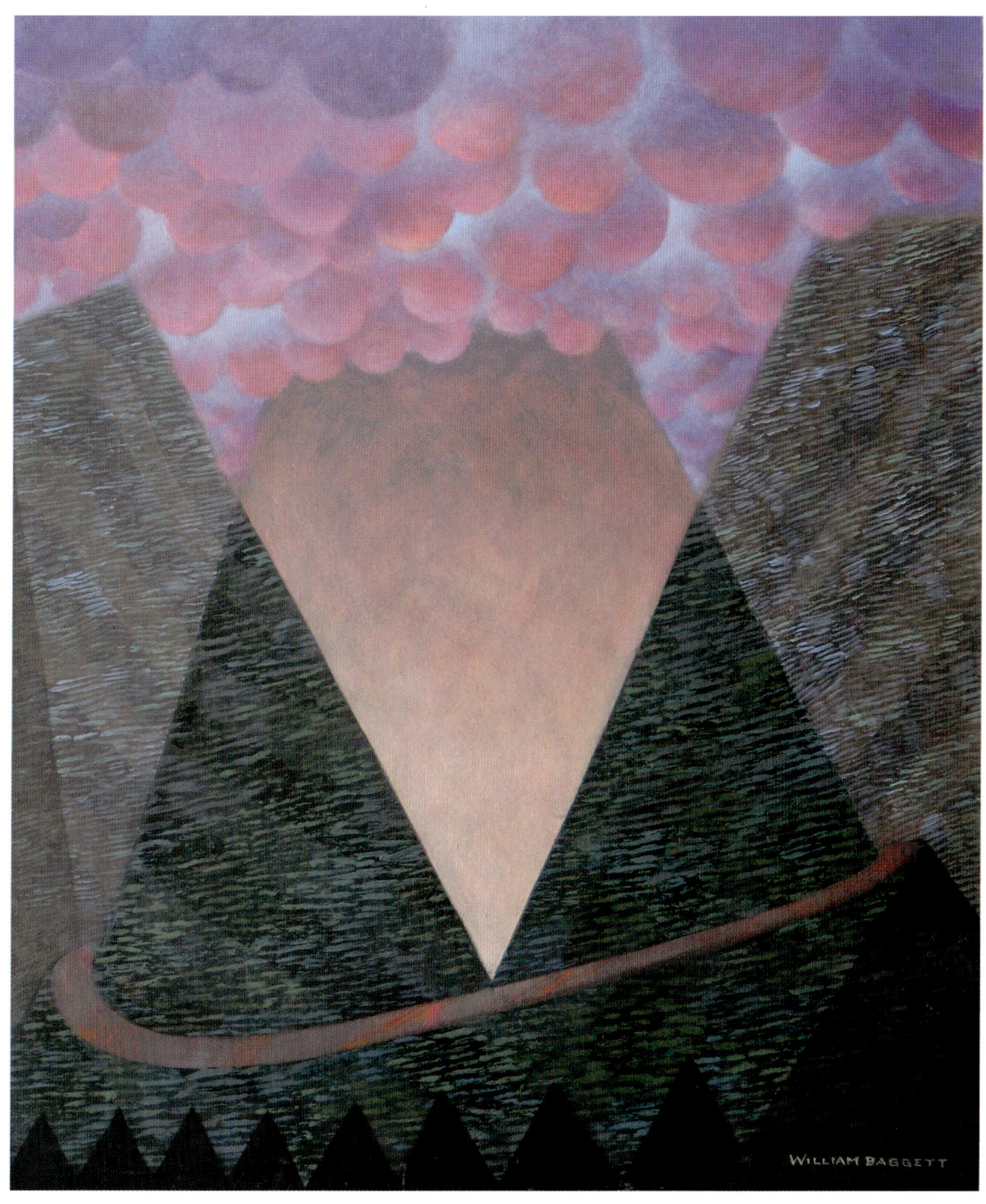

PLATE X. *Mammatus Birth*, 20″ x 24″

Cezanne reacted to the Impressionist's rendering of the fleeting effects of light and on the evocation of a specific moment in time by concentrating the eye on carefully orchestrated tableaus, each object a carefully articulated form through subtle transitions of warm and cool colors. Matisse formulated a different approach to painting which involved rendering the "essential character" of things, to distill the essential properties of things into abstract images of them and rendering them out of time. The 20th century witnessed the rise of Cubism and related conceptual art styles as well as Surrealism, both perhaps a variant of the timeless absolute sought by Matisse.

On the surface, Baggett seems to follow most closely Matisse towards presenting things as timeless absolutes. However, while Matisse's pictorial imagination apparently needed the stimulation of direct contact with things, Baggett works entirely from his memory — both visual and tactile. Because his memory is rich, complex and at times contradictory, the resulting images — as we have seen in *Trolling for Bodoni* — force the viewer to navigate painstakingly through the spatial construction, the dense layering of transparent as well as translucent coloring and the complexity of the implied physicality of things before the viewer realizes that what is seen is not transcriptions of the world but a careful arrangement of forms, lines and color, a construct that creates the illusion of depth, space and volume.

Baggett walks a very fine line here. Because his depiction of things is often painstakingly "real", only the complexity of the construction, prevents the juxtaposition of things to be perceived as surreal; i.e., as having some meaning.

Meticulous care and calm deliberateness are the dominant features of the paintings in this exhibition. The persona of artist and teacher merge to allocate shapes and lines, light, and color so that they are both aspects of reality and a demonstration of the inherent intent in Western painting: to create the illusion of depth, space and volume on a flat surface.

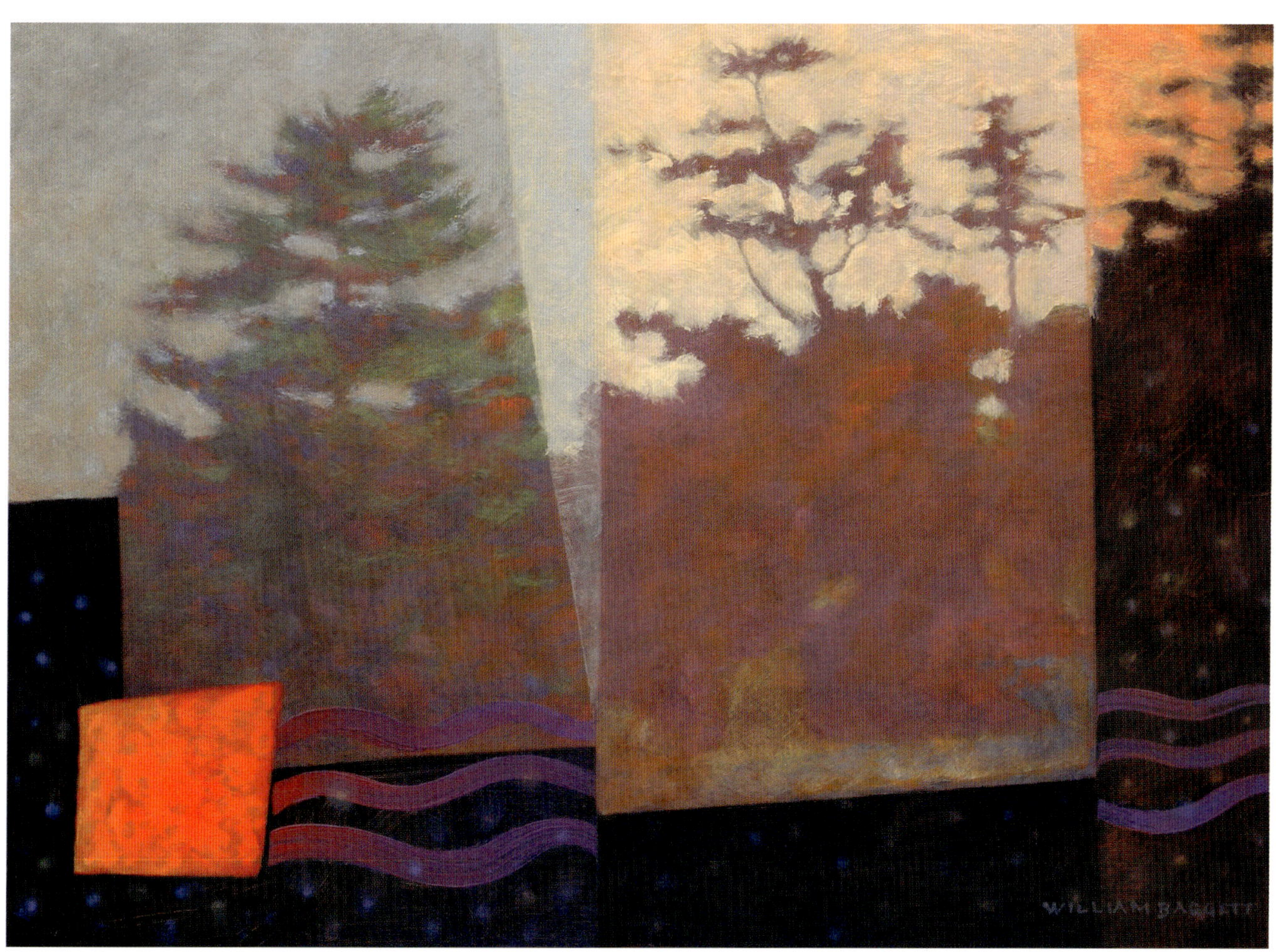

PLATE XI. *Evening Flow*, 16″ x 12″

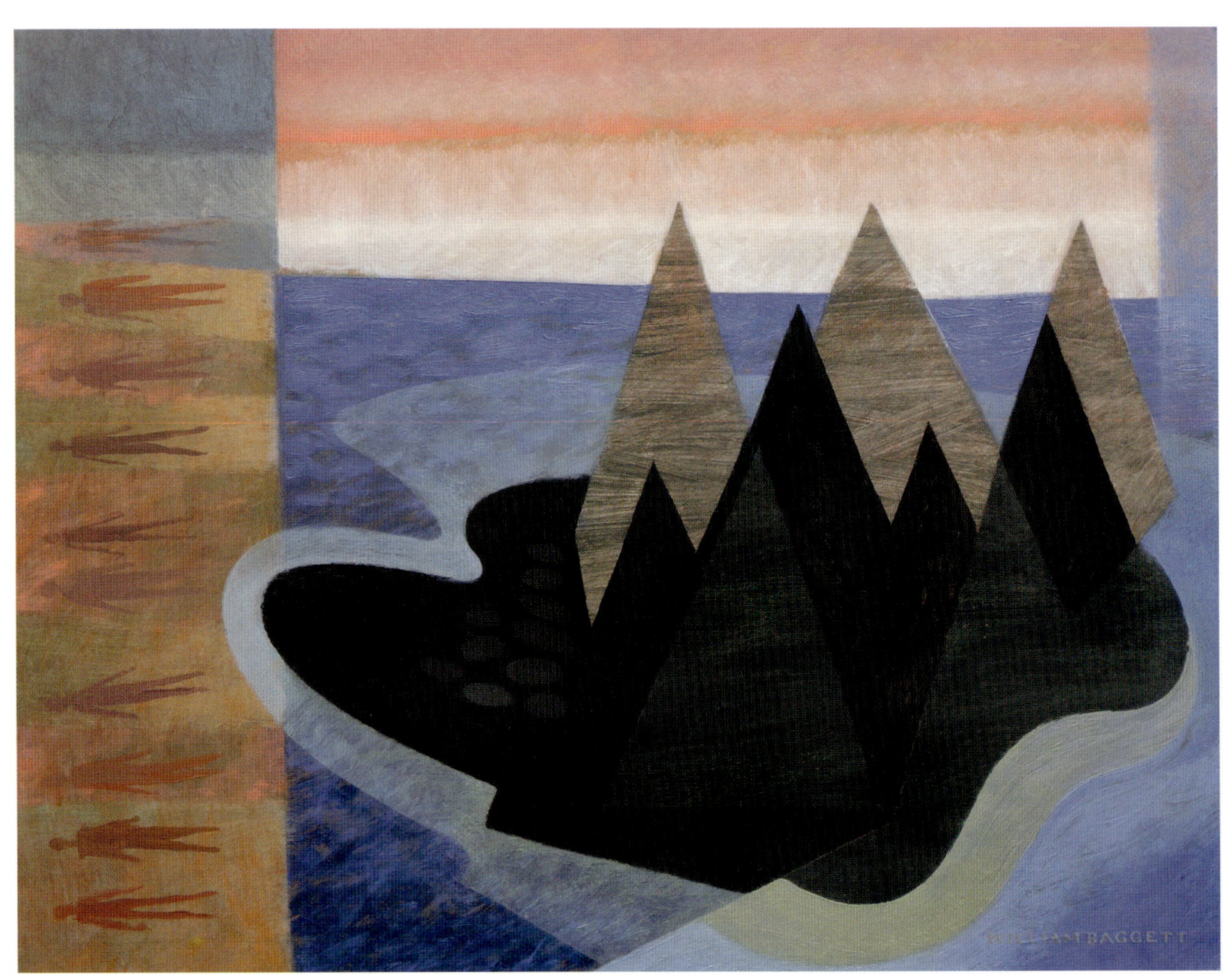

PLATE XII. *Islanders*, 20″ x 16″

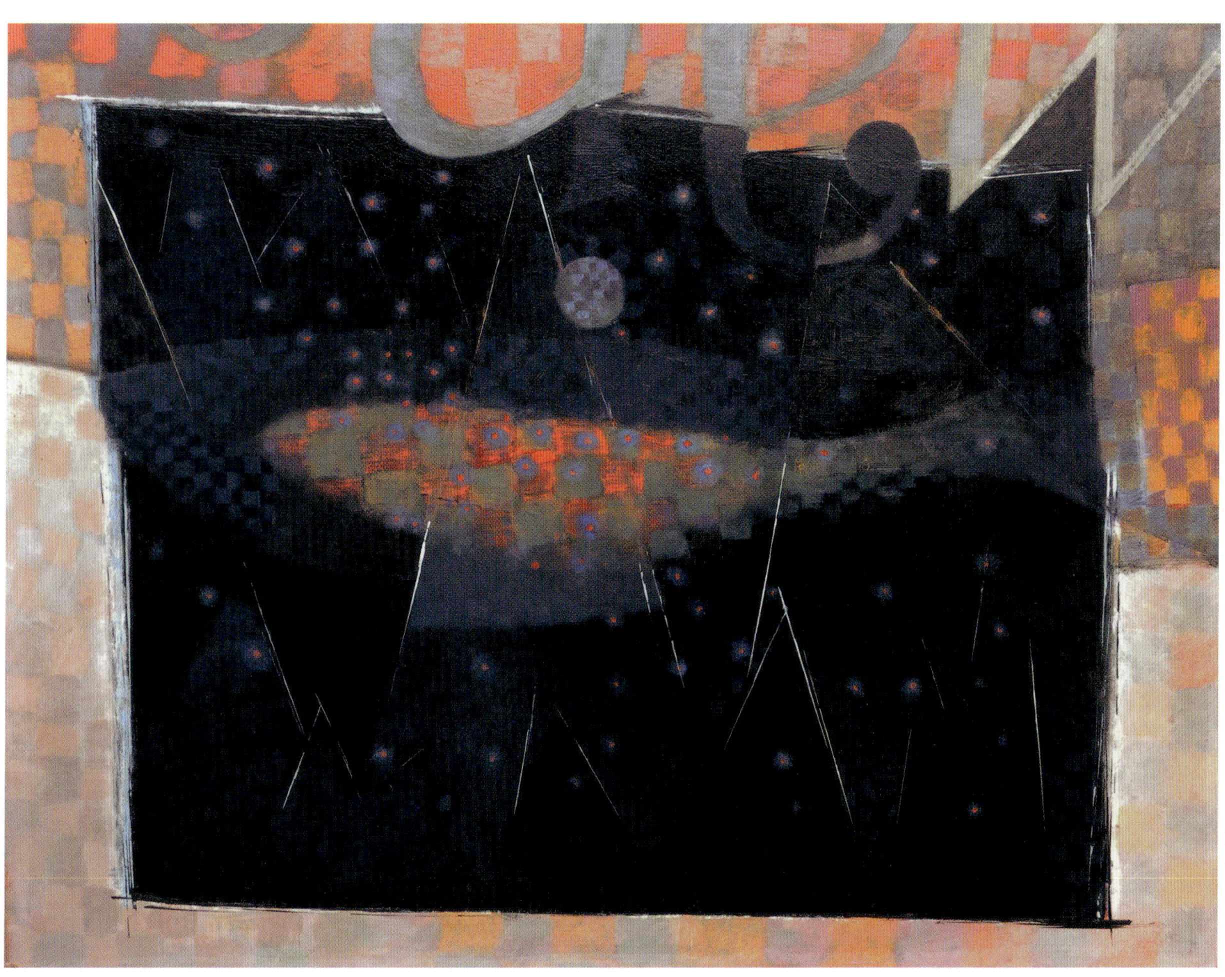

PLATE XIII. *Nocturne*, 20″ x 16″

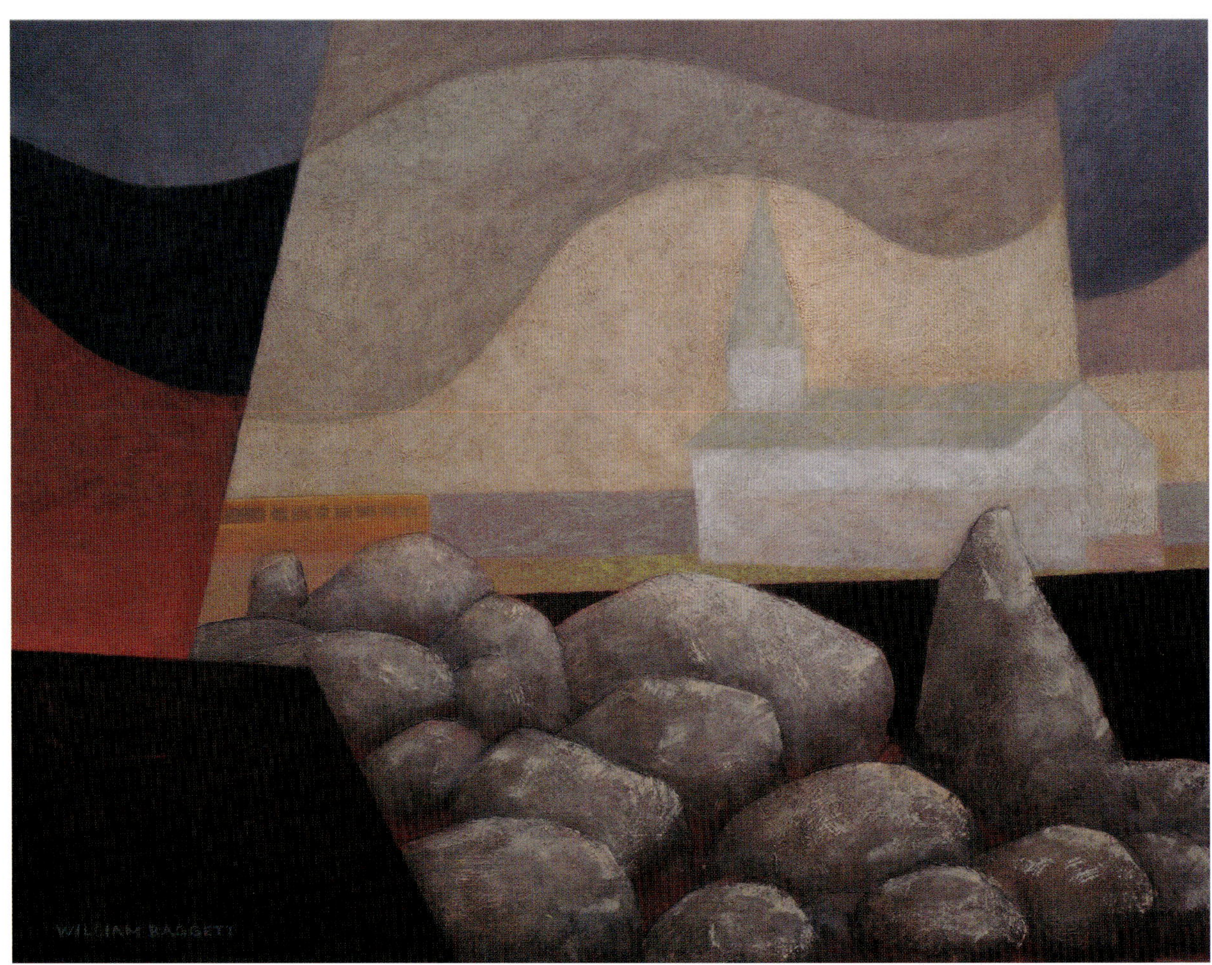

PLATE XIV. *Rock/Paper/Scissors*, 20″ x 16″

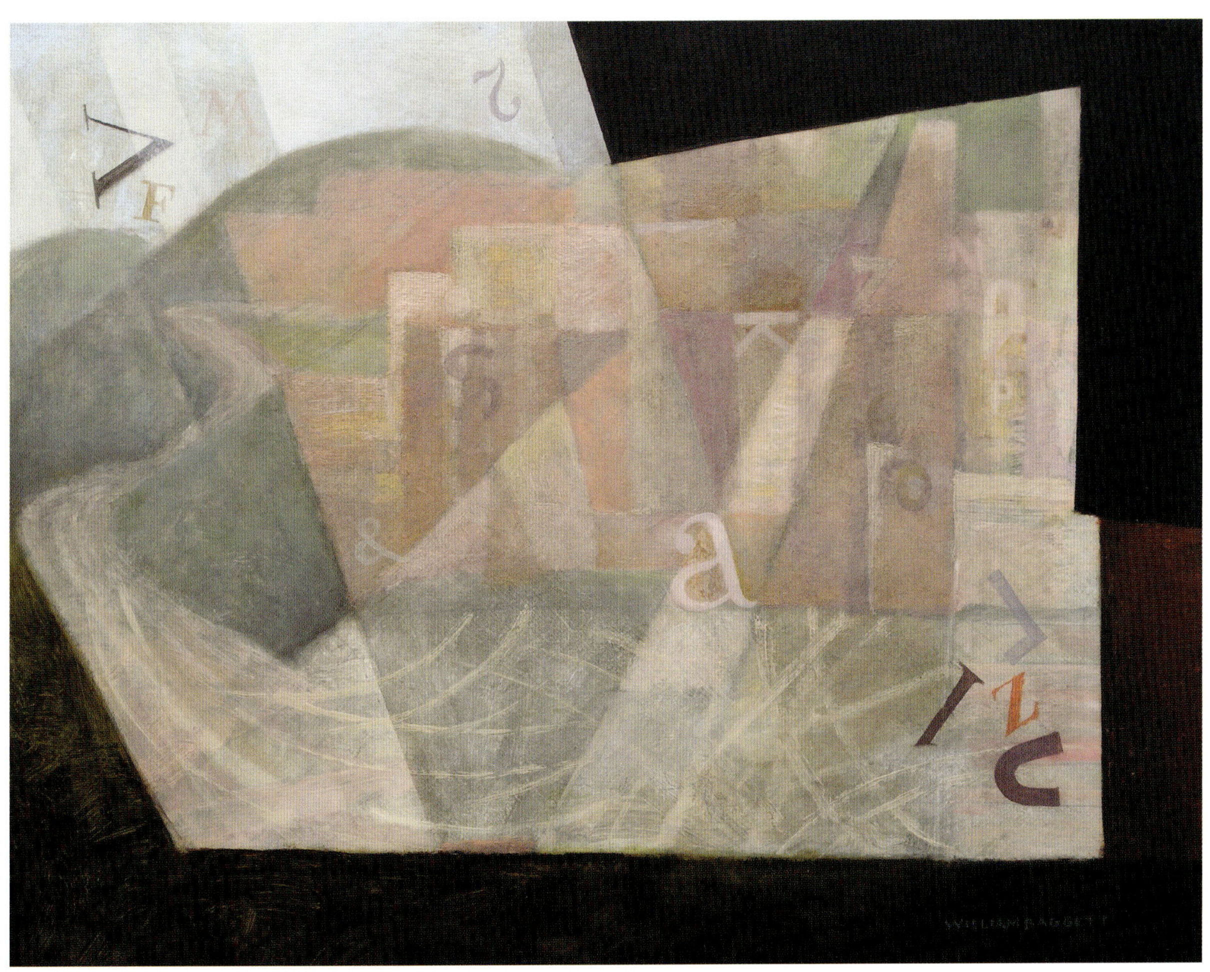

PLATE XV. *Sleeping Quarry*, 20″ x 16″

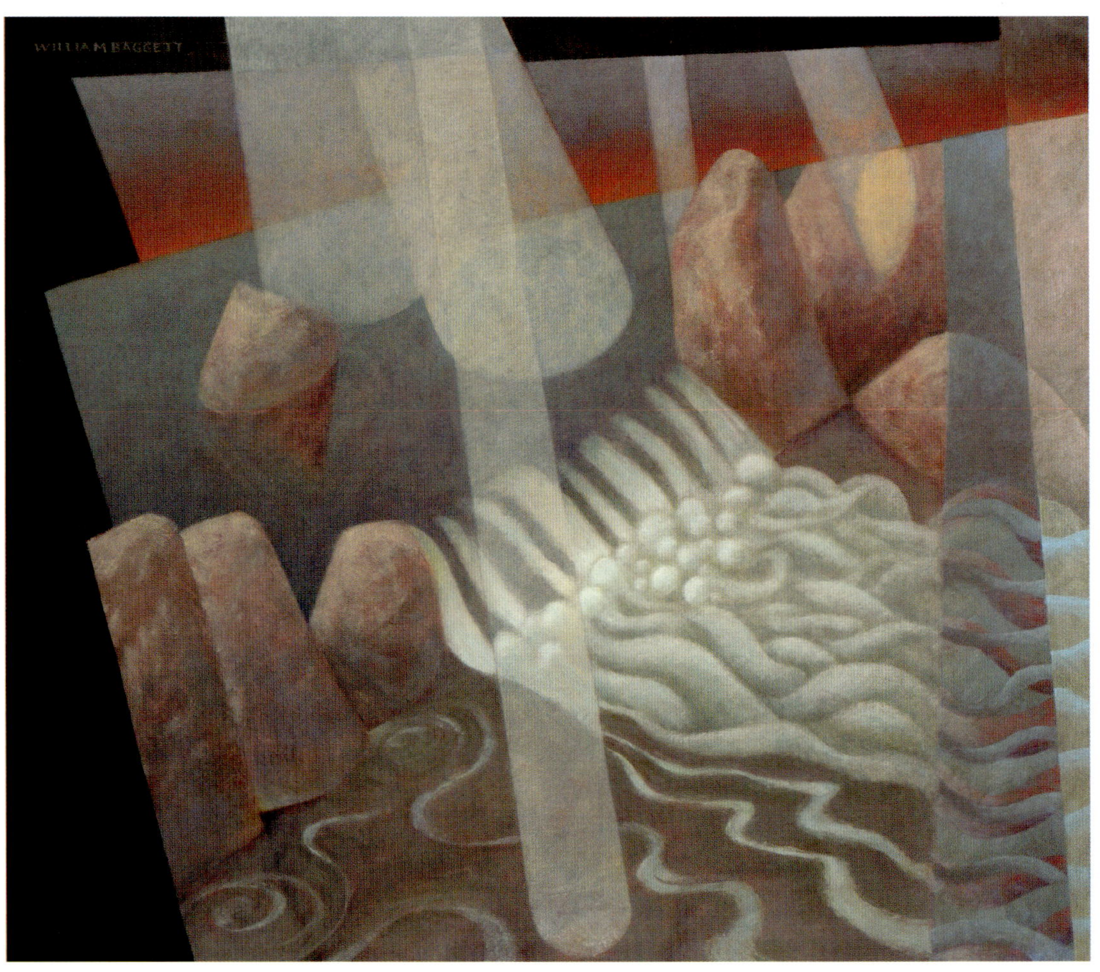

PLATE XVI. *Stream Analysis*, 22″ x 19″

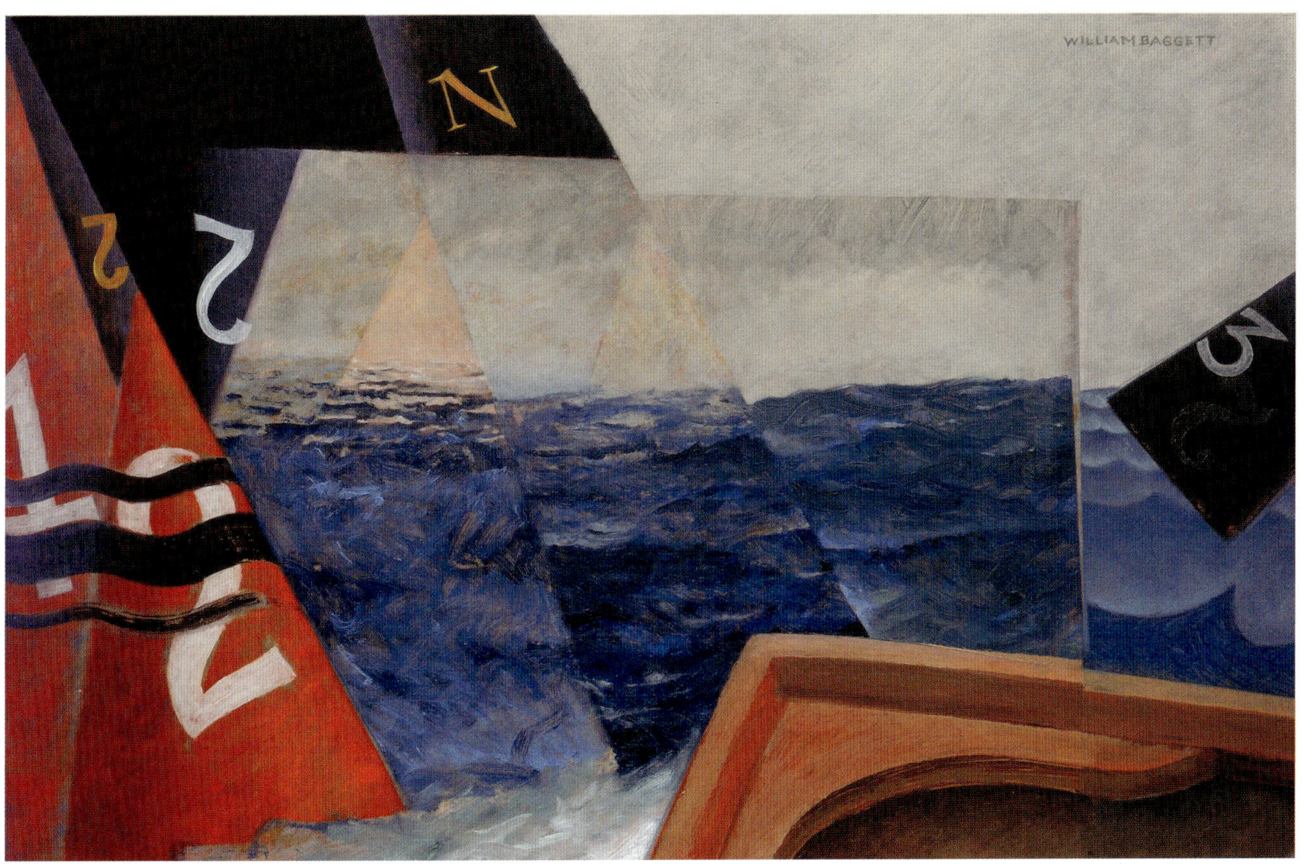

PLATE XVII. *Harbor Sequence*, 24″ x 16″

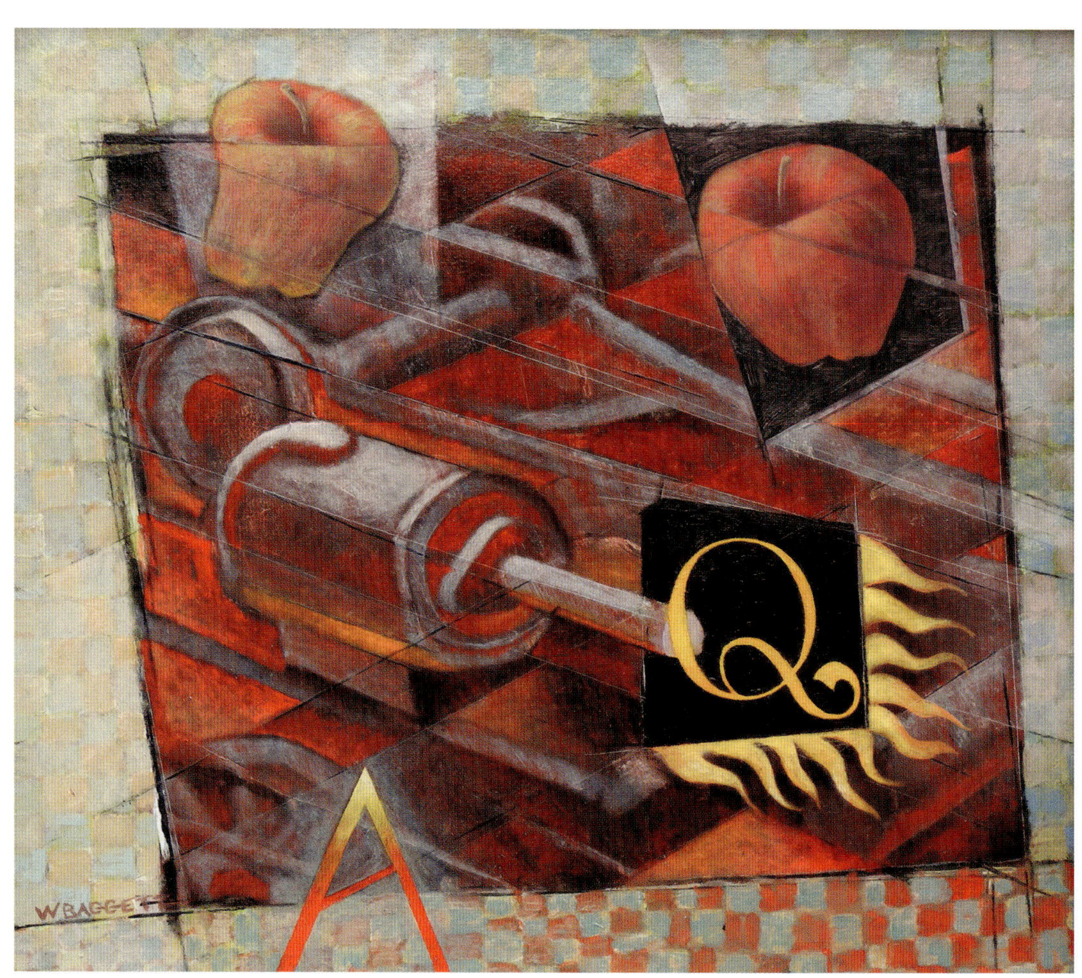

PLATE XVIII. *Vapor*, 21″ x 19″

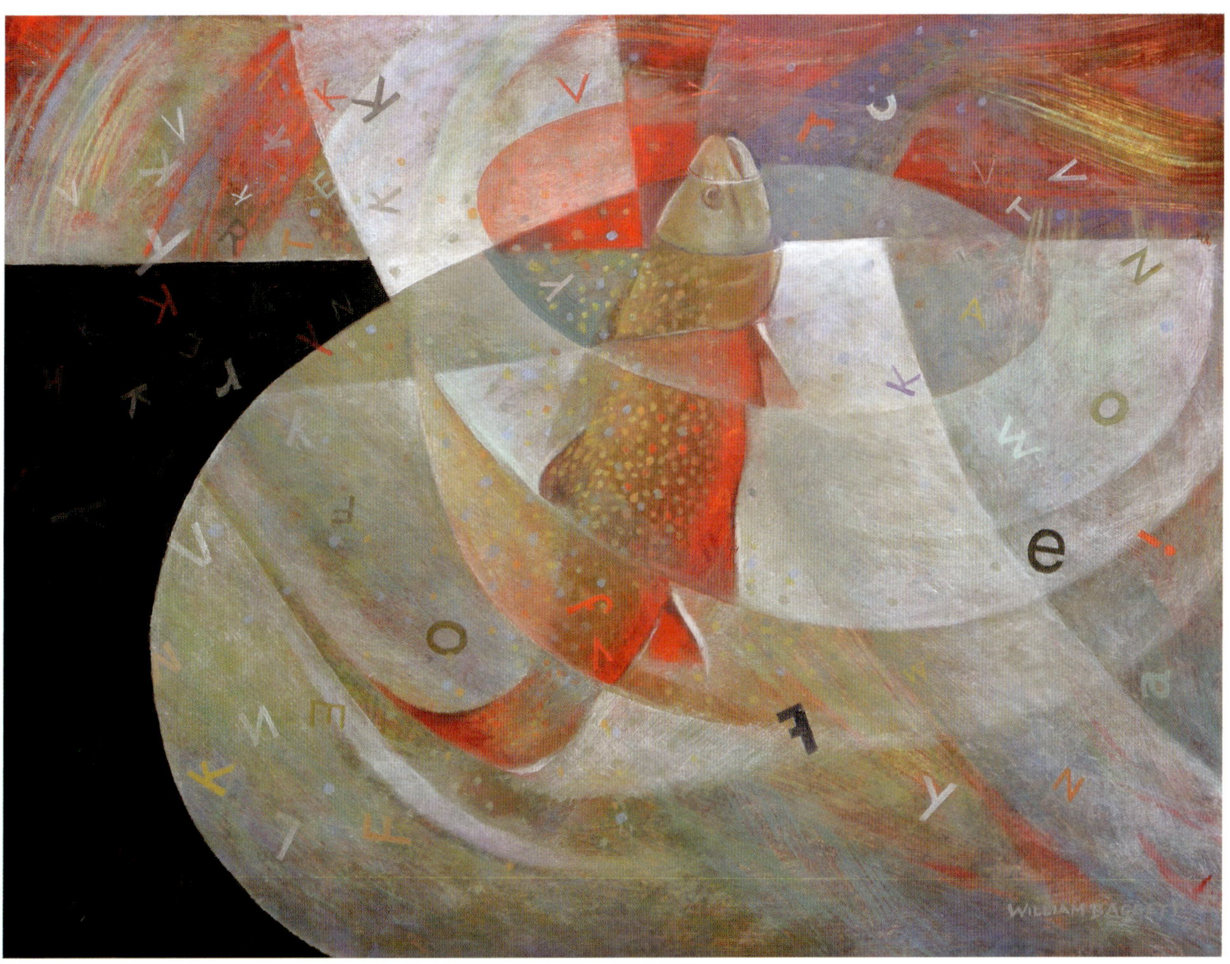

PLATE XIX. *Font Hatch*, 18″ x 14″

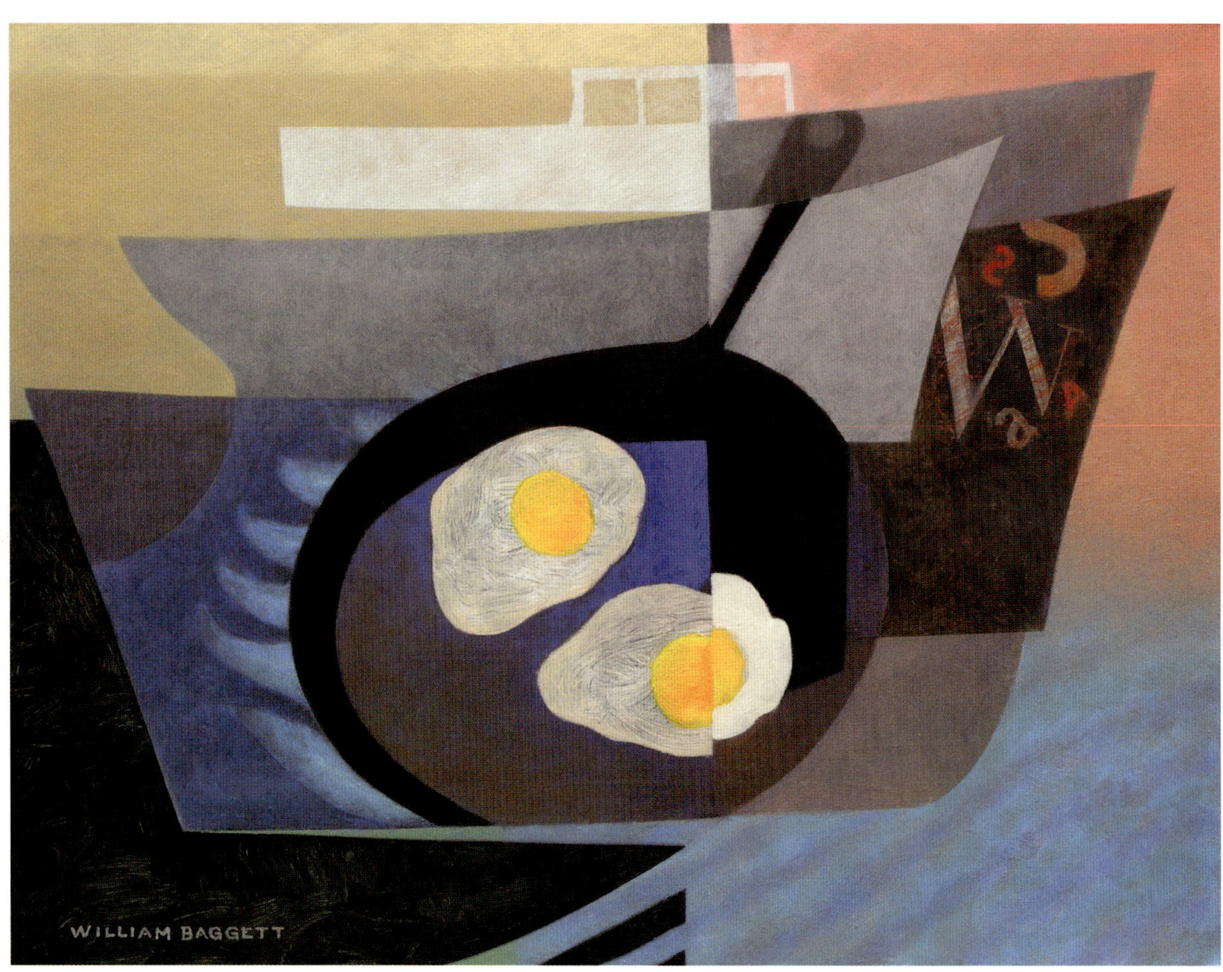

PLATE XX. *Galley*, 18″ x 14″

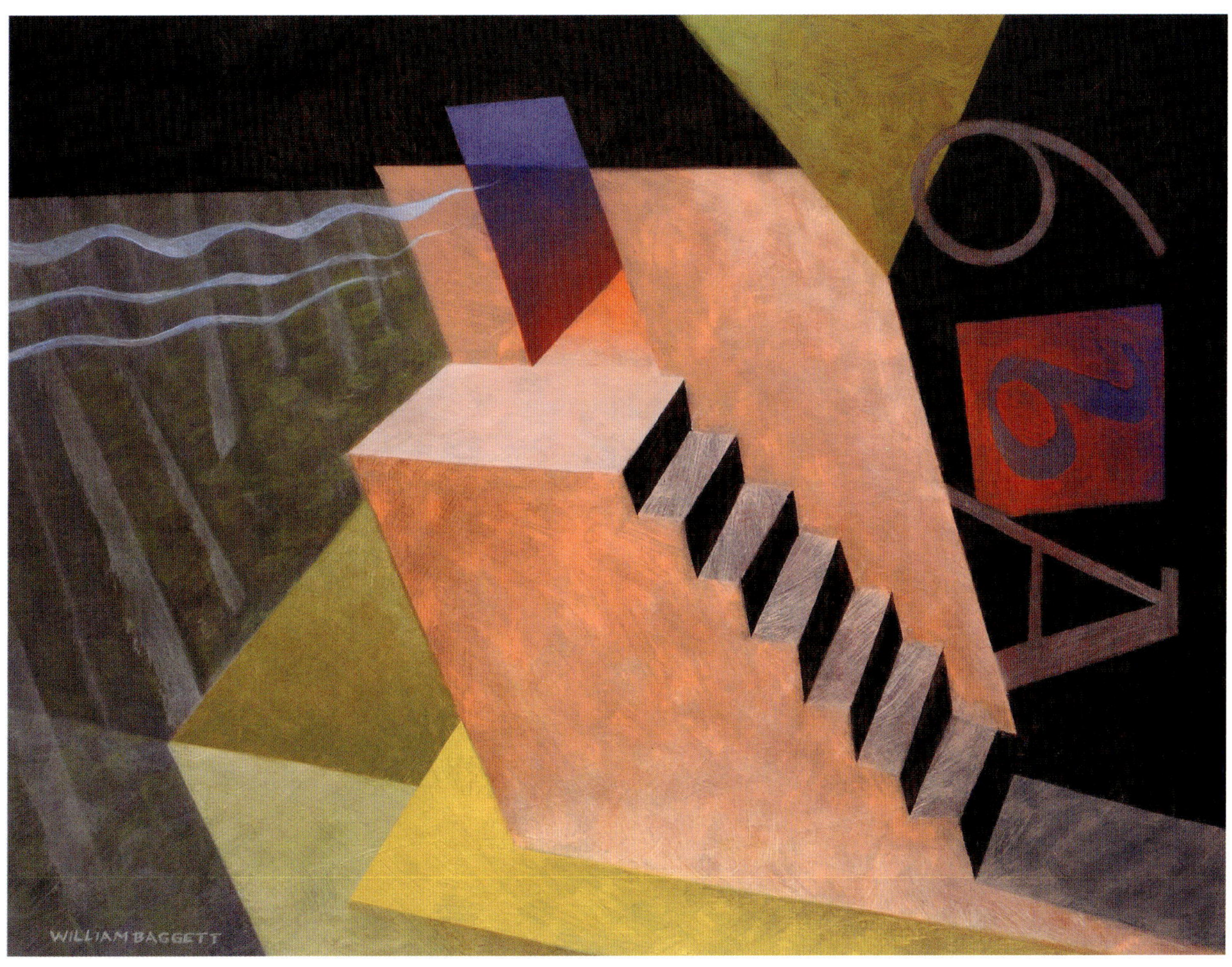

PLATE XXI. *Airing Cottage*, 18″ x 14″

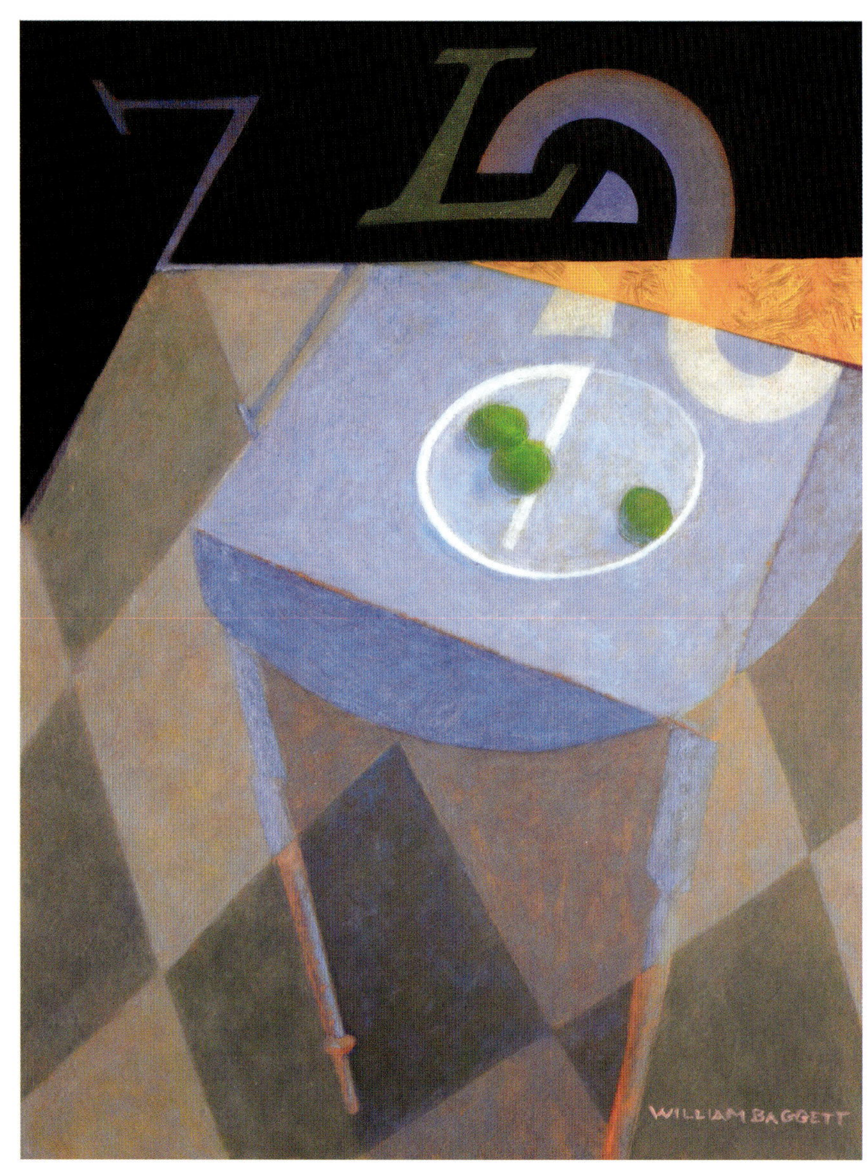

PLATE XXII. *Presumed Interior*, 12″ x 16″, 2010

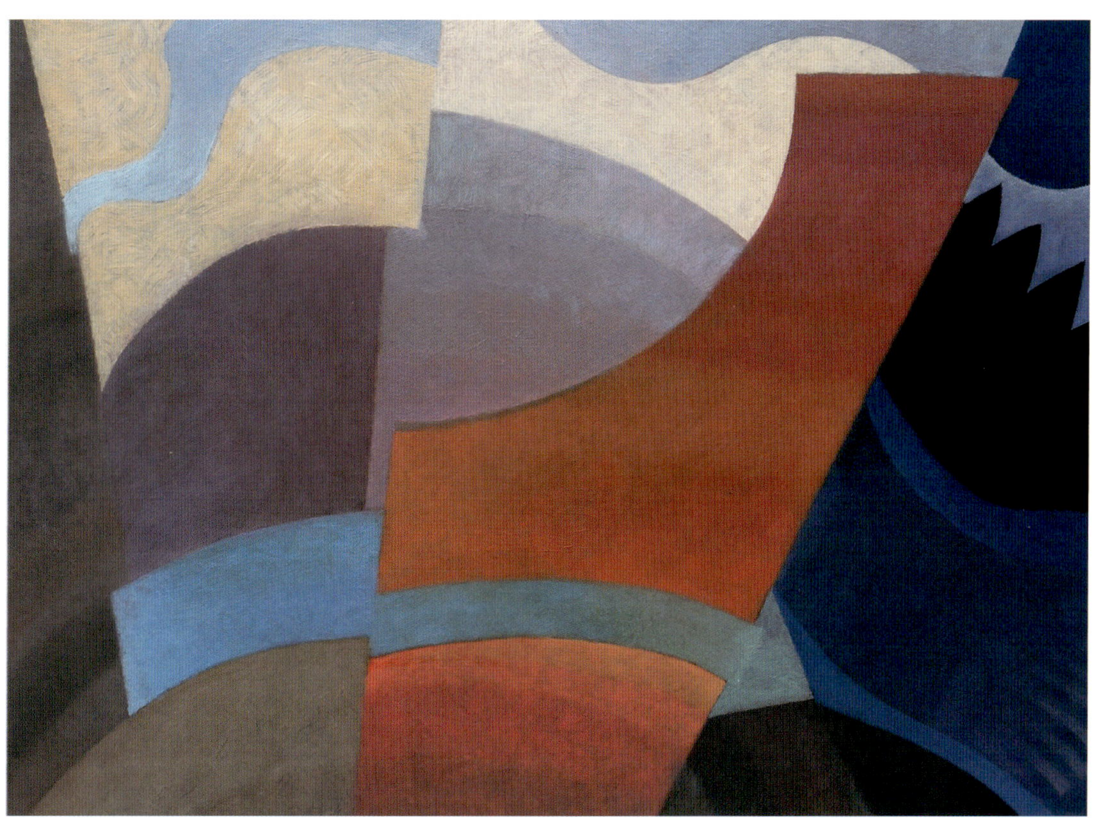

PLATE XXIII. *Time Zones*, 16″ x 12″

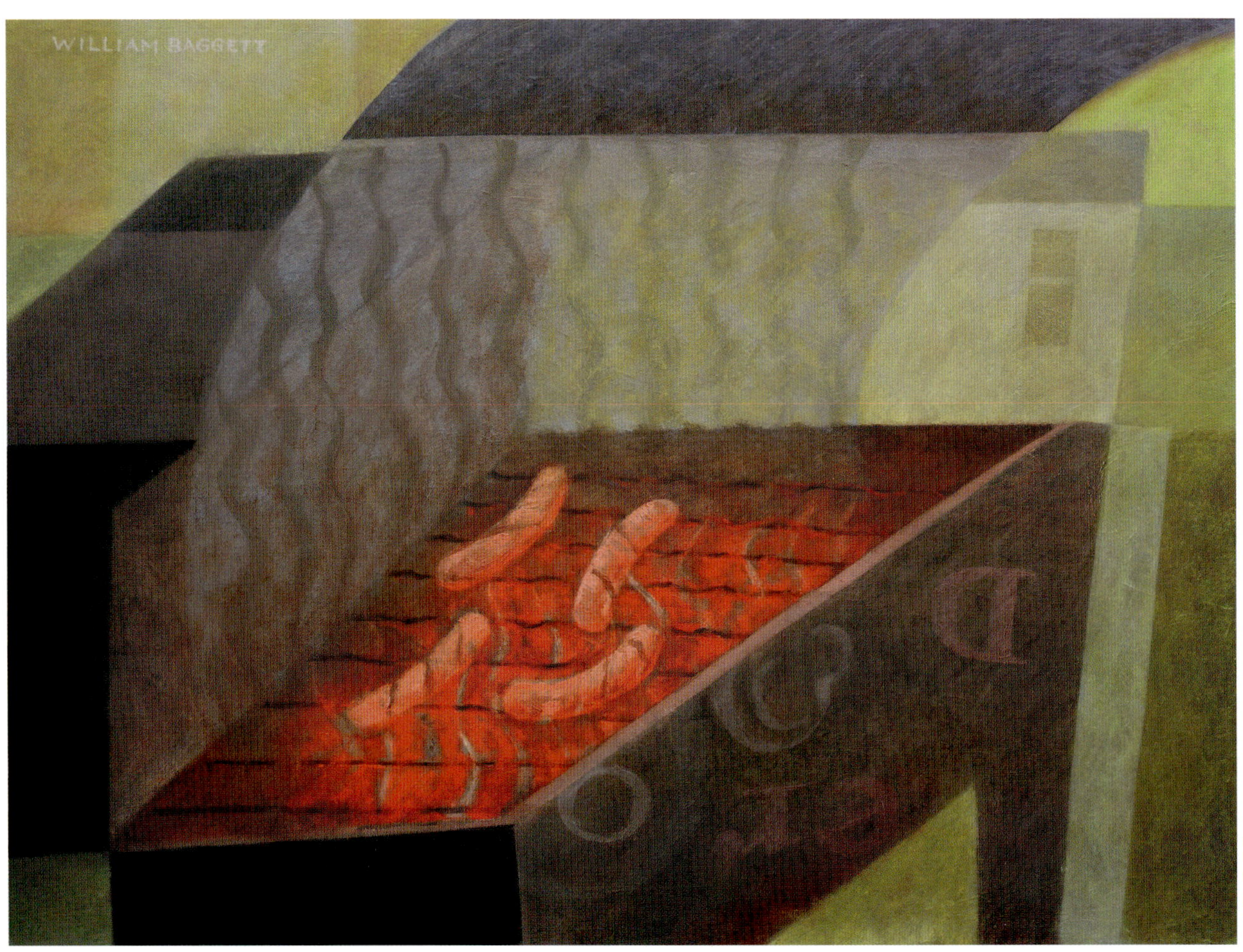

PLATE XXIV. *Backyard Motif,* 24″ x 18″

All works are executed in oil on panel.
Sizes (w x h) in this listing do not include frames.
** not pictured in catalog*

All images are copyrighted by the artist, William Baggett ©2010
Additional works and information about the artist
may be viewed at http://www.williambaggett.com

Overleaf: ***Font Hatch*** (*detail*), oil on panel, 18″ x 14″, 2008

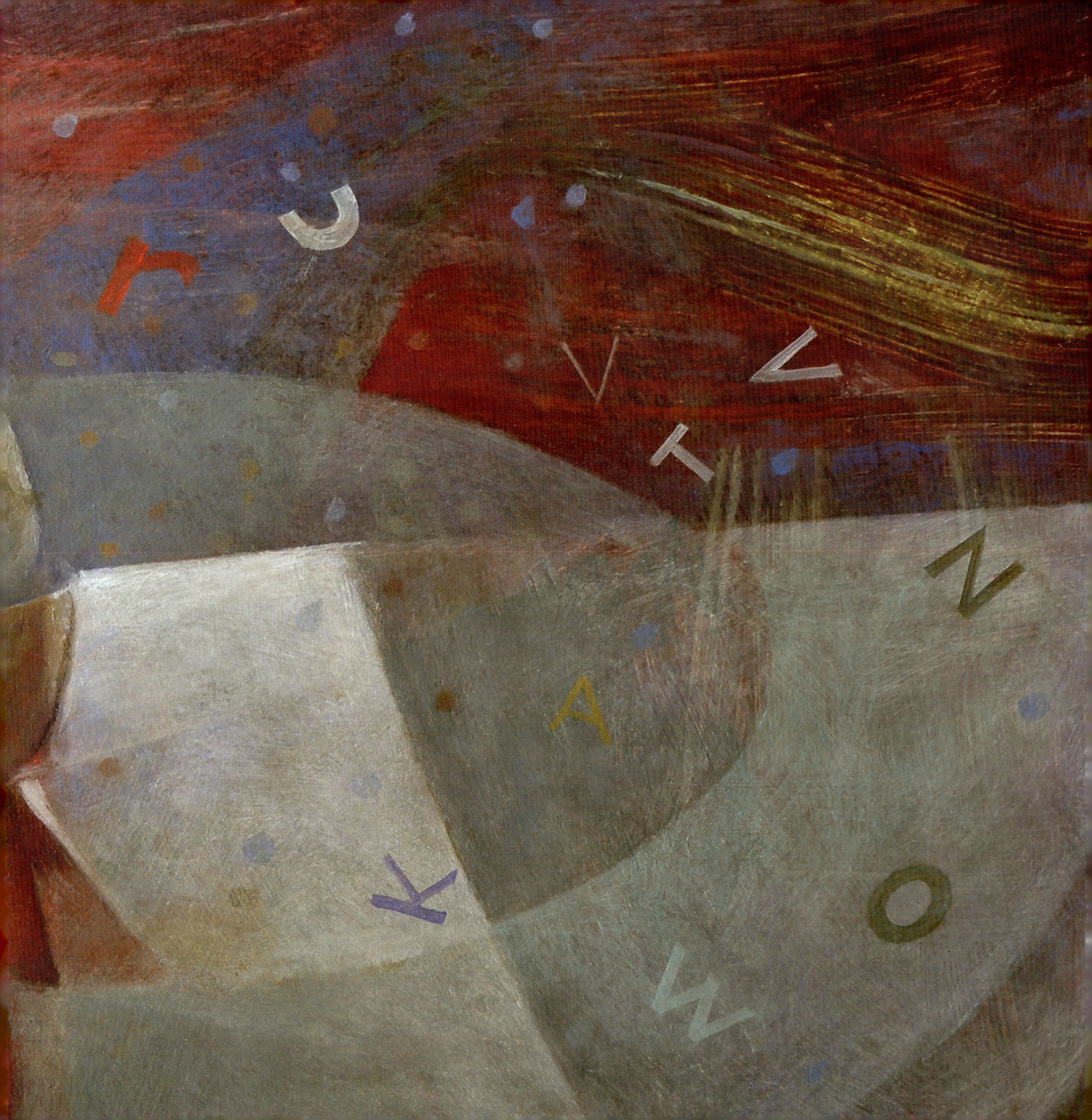